Sinning Saints

and their
Treasured Transgressions

Sinning Saints

Copyright © 2012 by The Moody Adams Evangelistic Association, Inc.

ISBN: 978-0-97259156-0

Scripture quotations are from The Holy Bible, King James Version (KJV) unless contained in quotations.

All rights are reserved by the publisher, but readers are encouraged to quote material from this book for reviews or teaching purposes, on condition the quote is not longer than 500 words and is not the primary content of a work being sold; that the contents are not altered; and that credit is properly given to the source. For additional usage guidelines, email the Publisher at: moodyadams@moodynews.com

Available from:

Web: http://www.moodynews.com
Telephone: 225-291-7333
Fax" 225-291-0103
Email: moodyadams@moodynews.com

Moody Adams Evangelistic Association, Inc.
11715 Bricksome Avenue, Suite B-3
Baton Rouge, Louisiana 70816

Sinning Saints

Foreword

I asked an active church member how she liked the visiting evangelist she had heard the night before. She replied, "I did not care for him. He used a lot of scripture nobody ever preaches on."

This book may well suffer a similar criticism; it is filled with scripture nobody ever preaches about.

It is important to understand two things in reading it:

One, the word 'saint' is used loosely, and technically incorrect in many cases. Since the Bible refers to all believers as 'saints,' you would have to accept present day church members as 'saints,' if you assume they are all true believers.

Second, the morality contained here is only for genuine Christians. Everyone else is expected to indulge in these transgressions. They are only doing what sinners are supposed to do.

Many believers will discover they are guilty of things they never heard were wrong. God will wink at this, but after learning what the Bible says, they must repent and accept God's cleansing and power of deliverance.

Sinning Saints

Table of Contents

1. Why America is Plunging Toward God's Judgment   5
2. Gambling, the Senseless Sin   13
3. Beer, Booze and Sipping Saints   31
4. Tattoos: Graffiti on God's Temple   55
5. The Evils of Immodest Dress   69
6. Liars Who Profess the Lord   75
7. Hooking up, Shacking up and Fooling Around   83
8. Tolerance and the Downfall of America   103
9. On Friendship With the World (by John Wesley)   129

Sinning Saints

1

Why America is Plunging Toward God's Judgment

I was shocked to discover the Christian worker had carried a girl into his motel room. We were in an area-wide evangelistic crusade at the time. A nationally known singing group was providing the music. One night after the service, a member of the singing group took a local nurse into his motel room. I complained to the group's leader and he assured me the situation would be corrected. The next morning the young woman's car was still at the man's room. I rushed to their leader and informed him they had failed to correct this problem.

The music leader responded rapidly with total shock at my complaint, he said, "He is not married."

I faced the stunning reality that fornication' by the unmarried had become accepted and approved in our country, even among Christians, even among Christian workers.

America is falling the same way God's favorite nation fell

Israel, God's chosen nation, forgot about the Lord's commandments and hurried on her sins. "My people are destroyed for lack of knowledge: because thou hast rejected knowledge, I will also reject

Sinning Saints

thee, that thou shalt be no priest to me: seeing thou hast forgotten the law of thy God, I will also forget thy children" (Hosea 4:6).

The Bible pronounces the woe of God's judgment on those who call evil good, "Woe unto them that call evil good, and good evil" (Isaiah 5:20). There are a host of evil sins America's Christians are now declaring are 'good.' Thei dead conscience allow them to practice many sins without any feeling of guilt.

People living wicked lives are condemned and so are their nations. "The wicked shall be turned into hell, and all the nations that forget God" (Psalm 9:17). It does not matter what the people approve their wickedness is condemned by God.

Nations that turn their back on God are doomed. "For the nation and kingdom that will not serve thee shall perish; yea, those nations shall be utterly wasted" (Isaiah 60:12). It is just a matter of time before nations that turn from Christ and wallow in wickedness are doomed.

The Bible is rejected as authoritative

Past generations have chosen the Bible as the final authority in matters of right and wrong. A new generation has chosen their intellect and feelings as the final authority in matters of right and wrong. "The Bible says," is being replaced by, "I do not feel there is anything wrong with this," or "I do not think this is wrong."
Right and wrong are not subjective matters. This is even true in human courts. Laws declare what is wrong. A judge is not at all influence by what a suspect thinks or feels. When we stand before God, He will give no consideration to what we thought or felt regarding right and wrong.

Sinning Saints

Conscience is easily 'seared' meaning they can sin without any feelings of guilt, "Speaking lies in hypocrisy; having their conscience seared with a hot iron" (I Timothy 4:2).

This generation is rushing toward the judgment of God and terrible ruin because they have not made the Word of God their supreme authority. This enables them to enjoy theirr wickedness with no sense of guilt.

Christians are firmly against sin. But many define sin differently than the Bible defines it. They passionately pursue these sins, declaring them all right, totally ignoring what the Bible says.

Why there is no revival

Churches are holding days of prayer for the nation. Some are indulging in a day of fasting and prayer. Yet no revival comes? Instead Christianity in America is in dangerous decline. Why? A favorite verse of this generation is this promise, made to the Jews in the Old Testament, "If my people, which are called by my name, will turn from their wicked ways..." "Wicked ways!" This is not even discussed. No one seems conscious of any wicked ways. There certainly is not national mourning and repentance of any "wicked ways."

Fifty years ago I remember having 'confession services' that were astonishing. A serviceman in Pensacola confessed he had stolen all his furniture off of the base. He wept, confessed and carried all the furniture back to his base. That night he and his wife slept on the floor. Another man confessed he had lied on an accident report, saying he was going the speed limit when he was far exceeding it. He

Sinning Saints

returned the money the insurance company had paid him.

In Texas I saw wide spread confession and repentance. People brought pornography and a pile of sinful things. On Sunday night we had a massive fire burning of the the sinful items accompanied by weeping confessions of sin. But I no long see or hear of such things, despite the fact that God orders it, "Confess your faults one to another..." (James 5:16).

There is no revival, despite all the prayers, because there is no repentance of sin.

Why prayers go unanswered

God does not even 'hear' the prayers of those living in sin, "But your iniquities have separated between you and your God, and your sins have hid his face from you, that he will not hear" (Isaiah 59:2).

"If I shut up heaven that there be no rain, or if I command the locusts to devour the land, or if I send pestilence among my people; If my people, which are called by my name, shall humble themselves, and pray, and seek my face, and turn from their wicked ways; then will I hear from heaven, and will forgive their sin, and will heal their land (2 Chronicles 7:13-15).

Why God's blessings are no longer on our nation

"The wicked shall be turned into hell, and all the nations that forget God" (Psalm 9:17).

Christians approach presidential elections as if electing a terrific president is the key to having a strong nation. The truth is a excellent

Sinning Saints

president is not the key, Judah had the greatest of leaders—Josiah. There never was king after him who was his equal (II Kings 23:23). Despite having a terrific leader, "the Lord did not turn away from the His fierce anger," and brought judgment upon the nation of Judah. The reason was they turned from the Lord and worshipped idols. Great leaders are not a substitute for a righteous people. "The LORD said also unto me in the days of Josiah the king, Hast thou seen that which backsliding Israel hath done? she is gone up upon every high mountain and under every green tree, and there hath played the harlot. And I said after she had done all these things, Turn thou unto me. But she returned not. And her treacherous sister Judah saw it. And I saw, when for all the causes whereby backsliding Israel committed adultery I had put her away, and given her a bill of divorce; yet her treacherous sister Judah feared not, but went and played the harlot also" (Jeremiah 3:6-8).

Christians must honestly search their hearts

Question: Do you practice what you preach? "Thou therefore which teachest another, teachest thou not thyself? thou that preachest a man should not steal, dost thou steal? Thou that sayest a man should not commit adultery, dost thou commit adultery? thou that abhorrest idols, dost thou commit sacrilege? Thou that makest thy boast of the law, through breaking the law dishonourest thou God?" (Romans 2:3). Do you teach one way and live another? Are you preaching messages you do not obey?

Question: Is your heart a harbor of hate? "He that saith he is in the light, and hateth his brother, is in darkness even until now" (I John2:4).

Sinning Saints

Question: Do you love your neighbor? I John 2:9 is quite straightforward, "If a man say, I love God, and hateth his brother, he is a liar: for he that loveth not his brother whom he hath seen, how can he love God whom he hath not seen?"

Question: Are you keeping the commandments Christ gave us? "He that saith, I know him, and keepeth not his commandments, is a liar, and the truth is not in him" (1 John 2:4).

Question: Are you judging people for things you are doing? Some Christians are judging other people as if they themselves are immune to judgment for their sins." And thinkest thou this, O man, that judgest them which do such things, and doest the same, that thou shalt escape the judgment of God?" (Romans 2:21-23).

"And why beholdest thou the mote that is in thy brother's eye, but considerest not the beam that is in thine own eye? Or how wilt thou say to thy brother, Let me pull out the mote out of thine eye; and, behold, a beam is in thine own eye? Thou hypocrite, first cast out the beam out of thine own eye; and then shalt thou see clearly to cast out the mote out of thy brother's eye" (Matthew 7:3-5).

Christians are called to live holy, pure, clean lives, "For God hath not called us unto uncleanness, but unto holiness" (I Thessalonians 4:7). When we are born again we are created to live holy, "And that ye put on the new man, which after God is created in righteousness and true holiness" (Ephesians 4:24).

"But now being made free from sin, and become servants to God, ye have your fruit unto holiness, and the end everlasting life" (Romans 6:22). We are not perfect, but neither are we in the bondage of sin as

Sinning Saints

we were before we were converted.

"Oh that my head were waters, and mine eyes a fountain of tears, that I might weep day and night for the slain of the daughter of my people!" (Jeremiah 9:1).

To read God's words about holy living and to look at the immoral lives of today's so called 'saints,' is enough to break our hearts as it did Jeremiah's. "Mine heart within me is broken because of the prophets; all my bones shake; I am like a drunken man, and like a man whom wine hath overcome, because of the LORD, and because of the words of his holiness. For the land is full of adulterers; for because of swearing the land mourneth; the pleasant places of the wilderness are dried up, and their course is evil, and their force is not right. For both prophet and priest are profane; yea, in my house have I found their wickedness, saith the LORD. Wherefore their way shall be unto them as slippery ways in the darkness: they shall be driven on, and fall therein: for I will bring evil upon them, even the year of their visitation, saith the LORD." (Jeremiah 23:9-12).

Jesus lamented the wickedness of people of Jerusalem, particularly over the religious leaders, "O Jerusalem, Jerusalem, thou that killest the prophets, and stonest them which are sent unto thee, how often would I have gathered thy children together, even as a hen gathereth her chickens under her wings, and ye would not" (Matthew 23:37). Today, He is weeping over the wickedness of Americans, particularly over the Christians."

If American Christians were to awaken from their slumber and face their own wickedness, they would join Christ in His sorrow—weeping over the wickedness that is prevailing in the land.

Sinning Saints

There is one last hope of America escaping judgment. That is massive repentance of sins throughout the nation.

In the following chapters I have listed a few of the sins the church is tolerating, even enjoying. These are some of the things Americans must repent of while there is still a little time before judgment.

Sinning Saints

2

Gambling, the Stupid Sin

Boxer Floyd Maywather lost $3 million betting on a single football game. The boxing champ, who has a passion for gambling, bet $3 million on the game between the University of Michigan and Alabama. According to Media Take Out, Floyd placed a bet that Michigan would win or lose by less than 15 points- however, he guessed wrong and lost $3 million after Alabama defeated Michigan 41-14. Mayweather can whip opponents in the ring, but he cannot whip the covetousness that drives him to get more and more money. "Gambling is the entertainment growth industry in this country. Before the late-1980s, legalized casinos existed in Nevada and Atlantic City. Today, 37 states plus the District of Columbia operate lotteries, and 48 states have some form of legalized gambling." (Eric Olsen, http://blogcritics.org/politics/article/lottery-state-sponsored-evil/).

Nobody can make sin look as lovely as the gambling industry can. They use neon lights, exciting sounds and synthetic casinos fronts. their backyard is filled with broken homes and dead men's bones.

When you enter many casinos they will even ask if you want to install the casino software on your computer. They want to turn your living room into another gambling casino!

All gambling casinos, whether online or in Las Vegas, deceitfully want to make you feel like you are having a terrific time.

Sinning Saints

Television has brought poker into our living rooms and made celebrities out of the winners. The gamblers entice people by advertising with pictures of new homes, vacation getaways, and talk of becoming a millionaire. I knew a gambler who won a widow's house in an Arkansas poker game. He had it moved before daybreak! Gamblers are not in the business of getting you a house or a vacation. They are deceivers out to take your house and anything else you own.

The gambling public, which includes about half of all Americans, declares there is no difference in betting in a casino and betting on the stock market. Wrong! In the stock market you are investing in a company that produces goods for people. In gambling you are investing in nothing. Rather you are taking money from the unfortunate when you win. In both cases you are taking a risk. Taking a risk is not gambling. You take a risk every time you get in a car or walk across the street. These are risks with a purpose. Gambling's only purpose is scamming the senseless customers.

Gamblers are throwing out nation-wide nets to snare new customers. "Come grab your $888 Welcome Bonus today!" says a promotion email sent out unsolicited. Another one says, They offer helpful 24/7 phone and live chat support team, fast payouts averaging over 97%." It also offers $300 free. All you have to do is just try their casino.

The industry is enjoying spectacular success. Americans spend over $54 billion on gambling every year. That is more than they spend on music, movie and video games combined.

Here is a startling fact. Betting websites are thought to number some

Sinning Saints

34,000! Only Utah and Hawaii prohibit all forms of gambling, all the others have some form of gambling.

The most corrupt form of gambling is the lotteries run by our government who is 'protecting' us from evil gamblers. Los Vegas advertises that their slot machines pay back 98 percent of what you put in them. Our protective government only pays back around 50 percent of money spent on lotteries!

Gamblers believe that if the public is stupid enough to bet their money on a Powerball Lottery where the odds of winning can be 100,000,000 to 1, they would believe the money is going to help "the kids." Gamblers try to justify their evil by saying revenues contribute to our nation's educational system. State legislators know lottery proceeds often end up in state's general fund. Then it is just another form of taxation, without any 'representation.' May God have mercy on a nation that has to turn to gambling to raise the money to educate her children!

Funny isn't it, the government taxes us to get money from the wealthy and gives it to the poor. They turn around and take from the poor to make one man rich, through their lotteries. In 2000, then-State Senator Barack Obama criticized the Illinois lottery on a Chicago talk show, calling it "regressive taxation," claiming it targeted "lower income" citizens who spent money they "don't necessarily have." He said, "The disproportionate number of people who consistently buy lottery tickets tend to be lower-income and working-class people, who can least, afford it. Even if they're not compulsive gamblers, they are probably spending money that they don't necessarily have.... The fact that the state systematically targets what we know to be lower-income persons as a way of

Sinning Saints

raising revenues is troublesome... This tends to be a form of regressive taxation" (http://abcnews.go.com/blogs/politics/2012/03/).

"Many of my conservative friends, who love to talk about Democrats and moral decline, never mention anything about gambling," writes Ellen Ratner. "That's because Republicans, like Democrats, are up to their necks in gambling money – both private, state and Native American."

A compelling, hard-hitting column by Esquire's Charlie Pierce about what it means to turn America into a casino republic, declaring, "The United States of America is now nothing more than a place where you gamble."

What is wrong with gambling? Well here are a few reasons no true Christian should ever gamble.

Gambling violates acceptable Christian stewardship

David wrote, "The earth is the Lord's, and everything in it, the world, and all who live in it; for he founded it upon the seas and established it upon the waters" (Psalms 24:1-2). God made it and He owns it. We are mere stewards handling God's money.

Adam and Eve were given a garden residence. The garden even had gold and other valuables (Genesis 2:10-12). When they sinned, they were driven from the garden and could not take anything with them (Genesis 3:24). It belonged to God, not Adam and Eve. Likewise, we are mere stewards of the money we have. If we waste money gambling we should ask, "Am I spending this as if I owned it, or as a good steward of the Lord's money."

To spend money on gambling is to ignore your stewardship, the heathen, the poor and the hungry.

John Wesley was a splendid example of good stewardship. Wesley limited his expenditures by not purchasing the kinds of things thought essential for a man in his station of life. In 1776, the English tax commissioners inspected his return and wrote him the following: "[We] cannot doubt but you have plate for which you have hitherto neglected to make an entry." They were saying a man of his prominence certainly must have some silver plate in his house and were accusing him of failing to pay excise tax on it. Wesley wrote back: "I have two silver spoons at London and two at Bristol. This is all the plates I have at present, and I shall not buy any more while so many round me want bread." (http://saintluther.blogspot.com/).

Gambling inflames the evil passion of covetousness

The 10th Commandment in God's Ten Commandments (Exodus 20:17), forbids covetousness. Covetousness is defined as, "Excessively and culpably desirous of the possessions of another." Remember, you do not win money from the casino; you are winning from others who have lost.

Living to make money is a game for fools, " For the love of money is the root of all evil: which while some coveted after, they have erred from the faith, and pierced themselves through with many sorrows," (I Timothy 6:10). You are only fooling yourself when you say you are just gambling for fun. You hope to make more money or you wouldn't be gambling.

Sinning Saints

Gambling proves you are not content with what you have, but are greedily trying to take other's money without doing anything for them, "Let your conversation be without covetousness; and be content with such things as ye have: for he hath said, I will never leave thee, nor forsake thee" (Hebrews 13:5).

"Covetousness is without a doubt the biggest sin in the world today," writers David J. Stewart. It is a sin God abhors, "For the wicked boasteth of his heart's desire, and blesseth the covetous, whom the LORD abhorreth" (Psalm 10:3).

Gambling is a legal form of stealing

Gambling allows you to take the possessions of others, legally. It is like two thieves getting together and each saying, "I will let you try and steal my money, if you will let me try to steal yours." It is a legal form of stealing, which violates another of God's Commandment: "Thou shall not steal" (Exodus 20:15).

"The lottery is nothing more than organized white-collar crime, and a voluntary tax on the stupid."

Dr. James Dobson, who served on the National Gambling Impact Study Commission, whose report was issued in 1999, cites these facts:
* Americans gamble more money each year than they spend on groceries!
* In Mississippi more money is spent on betting than on all retail

sales combined.
* 85% of young people have already become gamblers.
* Usually the people who gamble the most are the people who can afford it the least: the poor and the elderly (http://www.gospelway.com/morality/gambling.php).

"The United Methodist Church declares gambling is a sin which feeds on human greed and which invites people to place their trust in possessions, rather than in God, whom Christians should "love ... with all your heart"[Mark 12:29-30]. They quote the Apostle Paul who states: "But those who want to be rich fall into temptation and are trapped by many senseless and harmful desires that plunge people into ruin and destruction. For the love of money is a root of all kinds of evil, and in their eagerness to be rich some have wandered away from the faith and pierced themselves with many pains" (1 Tim. 6:9-10a).
(http://en.wikipedia.org/wiki/United_Methodist_Church).

Gambling is destructive to the work ethic

We are to earn our bread "by the sweat of our brow" (Genesis 3:19) not from rolling dice on a gambling table. For everyone who wins something at gambling, there are many, many losers—people who have been fooled by the enticing marketing appeals to part with their money.

You do not see many people driving Lexus automobiles standing in line to buy lottery tickets. "The dirty secret is that gambling preys upon the working poor, the people whose circumstances lead them to hope that, with a single scratch, all of their problems with inadequate health care, housing and social services will vanish,"

Sinning Saints

declares the website 'jesus-is-savior.com.' "Gambling creates a bad ethic—the vain hope that they can get something for nothing. Gambling destroys the connection between success in life and the real means of achieving it – hard work."

Gambling tends to corrupt the participant. Many employees have ruined their lives and disgraced their families by stealing their company's money. All too often the cause is traceable to a desperate attempt to pay gambling debts.

Stephen L Richards said that gambling "proceeds upon the assumption that one has to lose for another to gain. The element of chance in gambling leads those who indulge to believe that chance is the controlling and dominant influence in life. And so obsessed do some people become with it that they cannot contemplate or think of any other way in which to increase their means and their income except by taking the chance that gambling affords." (http://www.lds.org/ensign/1972/11/the-evils-of-gambling).

As gambling becomes increasingly popular in America, the value of an honest day's work is declining.

Gambling is an addiction that enslaves people

David Robertson, former chairman of the National Coalition Against Legalized Gambling, states, "Statistics prove that teen-age Internet gambling is the fastest growing addiction of the day, akin to drug and alcohol abuse in the 1930s. It's evil, for it feeds on those who are the weakest members of society—and that is the young and the poor."

Sinning Saints

Gambling stimulates the endorphin in the brain, causing an effect similar to taking cocaine. This is why gambling is addictive.
Dr. Howard J. Shaffer, Director of the Harvard Medical School Center for Addiction Studies, says gambling is worse than drugs, "Today, there are more children experiencing adverse symptoms from gambling than from drugs...and the problem is growing."

Richard L. Evans, a church leader in the early 1900s, said, "The spirit of gambling is a progressive thing. Usually it begins modestly; and then, like many other hazardous habits, it often grows beyond control. At best it wastes time and produces nothing. At worst it becomes a ruinous obsession and fosters false living by encouraging the futile belief that we can continually get something for nothing."
"Gambling's . . . sick legacy is its encouragement of pathological behavior. Gambling addicts – those who need the perpetual exhilaration of a bet – constitute 2.5 percent of all gamblers, although they account for 15 percent of all bets placed. In other words, the gambling lords depend upon their addicts just like the tobacco companies and drug pushers depend on theirs," declares Ellen Ratner a former White House correspondent.

"Opposition to lotteries first came in England in 1773, when the city of London petitioned the House of Commons to abolish lotteries because they were hurting the commerce of the kingdom and threatening the welfare and prosperity of the people" write Dallin H. Oaks, President, Brigham Young University. "In 1808 the Commons appointed a select committee to inquire into the evils attending lotteries. The committee report, which helped to abolish lotteries in England a few years later, is so current that it could have been written last week instead of over 160 years ago."

Sinning Saints

The House of Commons committee reported cases in which "people living in comfort and respectability had been reduced to poverty and distress; cases of domestic quarrels, assaults, and the ruin of family peace; and cases of fathers deserting their families, mothers neglecting their children, wives robbing their husbands of the earnings of months and years, and people pawning clothes, beds, and wedding rings, in order to indulge in the speculation."
"In other cases," the committee reported, "children had robbed their parents, servants their masters; suicides had been committed, and almost every crime that can be imagined had been occasioned, either directly or indirectly, through the baneful influence of lotteries."

John Wesley, in his sermon "The Use of Money," mentions in passing the taking of money from another via gambling as harming your neighbor and a violation of Christ's great commandment. He also would single out casinos as places that entice men and women to many kinds of sins. As such, no Christian who cares for the souls of those who visit such establishments should be in that line of business (John Meunier).

President Heber J. Grant said during his Presidency on September 21, 1925: "The Church has been and now is unalterably opposed to gambling in any form whatever. It is opposed to any game of chance, occupation, or so-called business, which takes money from the person who may be possessed of it without giving value received in return. It is opposed to all practices the tendency of which is to encourage the spirit of reckless speculation, and particularly to that which tends to degrade or weaken the high moral standard which members of the Church and our community at large have always maintained."

Sinning Saints

The late Thomas E. Dewey was governor of New York, he said, "The entire history of legalized gambling in this country and abroad shows that it has brought nothing but poverty, crime and corruption, demoralization of moral standards, and ultimately lower living standards and misery for all the people."

In 1962 United States Attorney General Robert F. Kennedy called attention to the overwhelming cost of gambling "... the American people are spending more on gambling than on medical care or education; ... in so doing, they are putting up the money for the corruption of public officials and the vicious activities of the dope peddlers, loan sharks, bootleggers, white slave traders, and slick confidence men. Investigation this past year by the FBI, Internal Revenue Service, the Narcotics Bureau, the Post Office Department, and all other federal investigative units have disclosed without any shadow of a doubt that corruption and racketeering, financed largely by gambling, are weakening the vitality and strength of this nation" (Robert F. Kennedy, "The Baleful Influence of Gambling," Atlantic Monthly, April 1962, p. 76).

Gambling is like a cancer, corrupting everything it touches

Alcoholism is its companion evil. That is why you see the free drinks served at the casinos. Prostitution and narcotics are also tied right in with the cards and the wheels and the dice. An estimated 500 prostitutes operate through the summer in Reno (http://preacherstudy.com/gambling.htm).

Gambling encourages all matters of evil. Where gambling casinos exist you will find whores, booze, illegal drugs, and many other forms of evil!

Sinning Saints

"For the love of money is the root of all evil: which while some coveted after, they have erred from the faith, and pierced themselves through with many sorrows" (I Timothy 6:10).

The crime rate in Nevada, where gambling flourishes, is extremely high. "Robberies are five times the national average, auto thefts triple, and burglary and larceny double. From eight to nine hundred vagrants with prison records are arrested EVERY MONTH in Reno. One police official stated, 'Reno and Las Vegas collect all the human garbage from the other states,' writes Rodney Reyman (http://preacherstudy.com/gambling.htm).

Many gamblers are scam artist

In addition to the profits from gambling the people are also scam artist. "They send spam to all email users in their database congratulating them on their recent lottery win. Then they proceed to announce that in order to release funds they must part with a certain amount (as tax/fees) as per the rules or risk forfeiture. Another form of lottery scam involves the selling of "systems" which purport to improve a player's chances of selecting the winning numbers in a Lotto game. This scam is based on the buyer's ignorance of probability and random numbers" (http://www.jesus-is-savior.com/Evils%20in%20America/gambling_is_a_sin.htm).

State lotteries and casinos are merely 'feeders' to Las Vegas. They get you hooked, and Las Vegas finishes you off.

Eric Olsen said, "I have been asked to give my thoughts on gambling, which like most anything that rolls around in my head, I am happy to share. My particular animus is against state-sponsored gambling, i.e. lotteries, in which the general populace gangs up on the poor, gullible and stupid in the name of "education" or some other unassailable public good. This nostrum is nothing more than a regressive tax and an opiate for those least in need of opiating."

Gambling is rapidly addicting young people

"Children as young as 10 are battling serious gambling problems, a major study has revealed, reports (stoppredatorygambling.org/.) "

While the United States continues to ignore its public health problem of gambling addiction, the first national study of the gambling habits of Australia's youth has found a tenth of kids aged 10-14 fit definitions of "at-risk" or "problem" gamblers. And a third have adults willing to place bets on their behalf. Almost a third of kids aged 10-14 said they had played electronic gambling machines in the previous year, more than half had purchased scratch tickets." Online predators are going after teens for everything from sex to their money. According to the following article, there's "2,500 Internet-based casinos that lure teenagers with offers of free tuition and other prizes. It is creating what some call an epidemic of gambling — and debt — on campuses everywhere," The Boston Globe reports.

Sinning Saints

Greg Hogan, president of his class at Lehigh University, robbed a bank to pay a $5,000 debt accumulated in online poker. Hogan, 20, will spend at least 22 months in prison.

Bella English, Globe Staff, reported, "The Massachusetts Council on Compulsive Gambling, declares, "Teenagers have a problem gambling rate of 10%-17%, a rate 2 to 3 times higher than the general population."

A survey by the Delaware Council on Gambling Problems (DCGP) showed that more than 30% of all high school students gamble periodically. The study found that:
"43% of eighth-grade boys and 19% of eighth grade girls gamble!"

Gambling kills many of its players

Citizen Magazine published a study showing one out of every five of the 15 million addicted gamblers will attempt suicide.

Nevada, where gambling is legalized, "has the highest suicide rate in the nation!" (http://preacherstudy.com/gambling.htm).

The suicide rate amongst gamblers is 150% higher than average in the whole population."

Solomon Bell, a Detroit police sergeant, pulled out his service pistol and killed himself at a blackjack table in a city's casinos. He was drowning in gambling debts. A casino spokesperson explained: "It's not like Bell died some honorable kind of death. He chose to kill himself. We saw absolutely no reason to close down our business

Sinning Saints

and deprive our patrons the use of our fourth floor." The blood was quickly cleaned from the carpet and gambling was soon resumed (http://www.jesus-is-savior.com/ Evils%20in%20America/gambling_is_a_sin.htm).

David J. Stewart reported, "On Linda Raasch's dining room table lay a foreclosure notice and several letters demanding payment on overdue bills. Her electricity was about to be shut off. In the garage, Raasch's car was running, the windows rolled down. She was inside, poisoned by carbon monoxide. She liked to play video poker machines."

Congresswoman Cynthia McKinney says, "Living to make money is a fool's game which brings misery, 'For the love of money is the root of all evil: which while some coveted after, they have erred from the faith, and pierced themselves through with many sorrows'" (1st Timothy 6:10).

The Bible clearly foretold that the last days would be marked by greedy men only concerned about themselves, "This know also, that in the last days perilous times shall come. For men shall be lovers of their own selves, covetous . . ." (II Timothy 3:1, 2).

The casting of 'lots' in the Bible does not justify gambling. Lots were made of sheep's knucklebones, and the roll of those bones indicated a certain meaning. God's intervened and caused the lots to fall in such a way as to tell His followers what to do.

Sinning Saints

Gambling can condemn your soul

"Therefore thou art inexcusable, O man, whosoever thou art that judgest: for wherein thou judgest another, thou condemnest thyself; for thou that judgest doest the same things" (Romans 2:3).
And thinkest thou this, O man, that judgest them which do such things, and doest the same, that thou shalt escape the judgment of God? (Romans 2:3).

Church members who gamble are covetous people and as such should be disciplined, "But now I have written unto you not to keep company, if any man that is called a brother be a fornicator, or covetous, or an idolater, or a railer, or a drunkard, or an extortioner; with such an one no not to eat" (I Corinthians 5:11).

Christians should not even sit down and eat with covetous gamblers. Remember gamblers never win money from the casino. Lottery ticket holders never win money from the lottery. They win it from other gamblers, often poor gamblers. The casino's bright lights blind gamblers to the suffering this game is inflicting on the poor. "There is a generation, whose teeth are as swords, and their jaw teeth as knives, to devour the poor from off the earth, and the needy from among men," (Proverbs 30:14).

Christians who gamble must repent. Until they do so, God abhors their covetous souls, "For the wicked boasteth of his heart's desire, and blesseth the covetous, whom the LORD abhorreth" (Psalm 10:3). Why does God abhor gamblers? Because for everyone who wins something at gambling, there are thousands of others who lose. They have been seduced by the gamblers to part with their money. Often the money meant they could not pay their rent, purchase food, or even buy gas to get home.

Christian—stop your gambling today

Christians must stop buying lottery tickets, playing bingo, betting on golf games, playing in casinos, gambling on sports events, betting on horse races, slipping a coin into a slot machine, and gambling on card games. These are gambling and gamblers are covetous people who are abhorred by God. Christians must not engage in the sin of gambling.

A man, In South Louisiana, announced to his pastor he would take care of the churches financial needs, for he had won the lottery. The pastor said, " no, you take the money back to the people you stole it from." Later the church accepted the gambling money and fired the pastor. Has money become the nation's god?

Sinning Saints

Sinning Saints

3

Beer, Booze and Sipping Saints

"How about beer with your Bible?" That is the question NBC's "Today" show host Campbell Brown asked March 4, 2012 on national television to introduce a article titled "Beer and Bibles: New Churches Lure Young Members (with beer).

Most Christians are familiar with the biblical story of Jesus turning water into wine, but now two pastors are turning a pub into a church complete with beer-drinking during the gatherings.

Pastors Calvin Culverwell and Vic Francis will officially turn Albany Sports Bar in Auckland, New Zealand into a house of worship on Sunday. After a years work, the Albany Sports Bar will officially serve as a church. Two pastors are turning a bar into a church and serving beer during the meetings which have no singing or sermons.

The sports bar service will not contain any sermons or singing, Francis said it will serve as both a place of prayer and a place to grab a beer.

Several beers kills 7 Christians

Brett Gerald, 30, of Greensburg, La. Celebrated his birthday, drinking four or five beers at a local country club, and then driving his pickup truck head on into Brenda Gaines' car.

In the Gaines vehicle were; her daughter Denise and Denise's four

Sinning Saints

children: Diamond Johnson, Jyran Johnson, Willie Gaines and Rogerick Johnson, Jr. A fellow church member, Angela Mosley, was also in the car. The group was returning home from a Bible study. Brenda, Denise, Diamond, Jyran and Angela were killed instantly in the crash. Willie Gaines was taken off life support June 3. Rogerick Johnson died Sunday, June 10.

State Police said Gerald's blood alcohol content was .15 percent, which is nearly twice the legal limit of .08 percent. This was Gerald's third arrest for drunk driving. It does not matter whether it is in beer, table wine, or hard liquor, alcohol in any form is a killer.

"Woe unto them that are mighty to drink wine, and men of strength to mingle strong drink" (Isaiah 5:22). Gerald understands what the Bible means by "woe." His woe is up to 200 years in prison.

Wine Country to Christians: 'We Don't Want Your Kind Out Here!'

In there is any doubt that alcohol and Christianity are at odds, view this article, "TEMECULA, Calif., Aug. 20, 2012 /Christian Newswire/ -- Calvary Chapel Bible Fellowship ("The Barn") is gearing up to file a federal lawsuit against the County of Riverside, California. in the event the County continues its ban on churches in the Temecula Wine Country, an area that is being expanded from approximately 7,000 acres to over 18,990 acres."

Trying to be a decent neighbor, Pastor Clark Van Wick met with a few vintners in an attempt to appease them, but was told, "We don't want your kind out here." (Lori Sanada, the Weekly Standard).

Sinning Saints

What Does the Bible Say About Drinking alcohol?

Proverbs 23:29-35 asks, "Who hath woe? who hath sorrow? who hath contentions? who hath babbling? who hath wounds without cause? who hath redness of eyes? They that tarry long at the wine; they that go to seek mixed wine. Look not thou upon the wine when it is red, when it giveth his colour in the cup, when it moveth itself aright. At the last it biteth like a serpent, and stingeth like an adder. Thine eyes shall behold strange women, and thine heart shall utter perverse things. Yea, thou shalt be as he that lieth down in the midst of the sea, or as he that lieth upon the top of a mast. They have stricken me, shalt thou say, and I was not sick; they have beaten me, and I felt it not: when shall I awake? I will seek it yet again."

If you have been around people who drink alcohol, you know they do it to get a buzz from it. They babble nonsense, while others laugh at them. They focus on female strangers, which has become the favorite sport of those who pick up women to fornicate. They say filthy, perverse things. They get nauseated. Yet, when they wake up, they go back to drinking.

Alcohol is the author of many sad stories

A Christian counselor wrote me the following: "I gave you three examples of "dedicated" church people whose life got messed up with alcohol. One example is the couple who were active in the church and the husband thought it "OK" to have a glass of wine. His wife did not drink and he persisted in his effort to get her to have a drink with him. She finally gave in and had a drink with him. She

Sinning Saints

became a raging alcoholic almost overnight. She was petite, pretty, and a joy to be around before she started to drink. She became sloppy, heavy, and flirtatious after she started to drink. They have lived apart often over the last several years.

"The second example is a couple who had been married for more than 20 years and was regular in church attendance. The husband was a "weekend" drinker and thought it was OK. Actually he was an alcoholic and his wife left him because of his drinking.

"The 3rd couple was active in their church. They were not drinkers but the wife thought it OK to have some wine with a male friend. This drinking led to sex in the backseat of a car. This was a mother of 6 and she and her husband had been leaders of music in the high school department of their church. These are people I have known and been friends with as well as a counselor with two of the men.

Alcohol is Killing America's Youth

Alcohol has killed five times as many college students as died in the World Trade Centers." Half the World Trade Center casualties are happening every year in our colleges," said researcher, Mark Goldman, a psychology professor at the University of South Florida.

As a result of alcohol-related injuries, 1,400 college students in the U.S. are killed each year.

Alcohol is a leading factor in the three leading causes of 15-24 olds deaths: automobile crashes, homicides and suicides. Each year, approximately 5,000 people under the age of 21 die as a result of underage drinking. This includes 1,900 deaths from car accidents,

Sinning Saints

1,600 from homicides, 300 from suicides. Hundreds of other deaths were due to accidents like falling and drowning.

A human being is killed in alcohol-related U.S. traffic fatalities, on an average of every 31 minutes (National Highway Traffic Safety {NHTSA}, Traffic Safety Facts, 1996).

Alcohol contributes to 100,000 deaths in America every year. It is the third leading cause of preventable mortality in the United States. Drivers under 25 were more likely than those over 25 to be intoxicated in a fatal crash (CDC, "Alcohol-Related Traffic Fatalities Among Youth and Young Adults – United States, 1982-1989," MMWR, 3/91, p. 179).

The number of drivers who have fatal accidents after drinking alcohol, is estimated to be 380 times higher than those who have not drank. (NIAAA "Drinking and Driving," Alcohol Alert No. 31, 1/96).

Those who murdered intimates admitted drinking the largest quantity, for the longest period, prior to the offense. (U.S. Department of Justice, Bureau of Justice Statistics, Alcohol and Crime, 1998).
Alcohol has many ways of killing our young people. Heavy and chronic drinking increases cancer risks, with an estimated 2-4% of all cancer cases believed caused directly or indirectly by alcohol abuse. (NIAAA, Alcohol Alert, No. 21, 7/93).

Colleges turning into bars
A significant new study reveals disturbing details about the dangerous drinking habits on college campuses across America. NBC's Robert Hager reports: "Researchers integrated various

Sinning Saints

databases and survey results to reach their findings. Motor vehicle fatalities were the most common form of alcohol-related deaths. The statistics included college students killed in car accidents if the students had alcohol in their blood, even if the level was below the legal limit. Students who died in other alcohol-related accidents, such as falls and drownings, were included. Those who died as a result of homicides or suicides were not. In general, drinking rates are highest among incoming freshmen, males, members of fraternities or sororities and athletes, a task force found." Colleges are frantic to enroll more students to increase their income. They are lowering moral standards to compete. Money is the reason.

The big problem: Binge drinking, defined as five or more drinks in a row for men and at least four for women. About 40 percent of college students binge drink, taking four or five drinks in a row.

An estimated 1,400 students aged 18 to 24 are killed every year in alcohol-related accidents.

It is estimated that alcohol contributes to 500,000 injuries and 70,000 cases of sexual assault or date rape, and 400,000 students between 18 and 24 years old reported having had unprotected sex as a result of drinking. Additionally, more than one-fourth of college students, in that age group, have driven while under the influence in the past year, the report said.

The above facts came from a federally supported Task Force on College Drinking, college presidents, scientists and students convened by the National Institute on Alcohol Abuse and Alcoholism. This institute is part of the National Institutes of Health.

What Alcohol Does to the Human Body

Alcohol is metabolized extremely quickly by the body, reaching the brain in one minute. Alcohol affects every organ in the body. Its most drastic affect is on the liver. It travels through the blood stream to the liver. The liver cells, are the only cells in our bodies that can produce enough of the enzymes that, oxidize alcohol rapidly (about ½ ounce an hour). While dealing with alcohol, the liver has to neglect the fat in the blood stream, which leads to fatty livers in heavy drinkers. This often leads to cirrhosis of liver.

It also increases:
- The risk of gouty arthritis
- The risk of cancer in the liver, pancreas, rectum, breast, mouth, pharynx, larynx and esophagus
- Heart Disease
- High blood pressure, blood lipids and the risk of stroke
- The risk of kidney failure
- Neuropathy and dementia
- Impairment of balance and memory

Alcohol kills more people than AIDS, TB, or violence

Reuters reports, "Alcohol causes nearly 4 percent of deaths worldwide, more than AIDS, tuberculosis or violence, the World Health Organization warned on Friday...

"Approximately 2.5 million people die each year from alcohol related causes, the WHO said in its "Global Status Report on Alcohol and Health." (World Health Organization).

Sinning Saints

Alcohol has four proven affects on the human brain.

1. Damages the brain of an unborn child
"Drinking during pregnancy can lead to a range of physical, learning, and behavioral effects in the developing brain, the most serious of which is a collection of symptoms known as fetal alcohol syndrome" (FAS, National Institute of Health, number 63, October 2004).
The brain goes through rapid development and "wiring" changes during the ages of 12-21. Drinking during those years can damage this development that is essential to brain growth).

2. It impairs judgment. Isaiah 28:7 says, "But they also have erred through wine, and through strong drink are out of the way ; the priest and the prophet have erred through strong drink, they are swallowed up of wine, they are out of the way through strong drink; they err in vision, they stumble in judgment."

Alcohol dulls the brain's alarm that monitors mistakes," a study finds (September 1, 2011 in Psychology & Psychiatry).

"Most people have witnessed otherwise intelligent people doing embarrassing or stupid things when they are intoxicated, but what specifically happens in the brain to cause such drunken actions? A new study testing alcohol's effects on brain activity from the University of Missouri says that alcohol dulls the brain 'signal' that warns people when they are making a mistake, ultimately reducing self control" (http://www.physorg.com/news/2011-09-alcohol-dulls-brain-alarm.html).

3. Leads to lawlessness. Habakkuk 2:5 says, "Yea also, because he transgresseth by wine, he is a proud man, neither keepeth at home,

Sinning Saints

who enlargeth his desire as hell, and is as death, and cannot be satisfied..."

About 3 million violent crimes occur each year in which the offender is said to have been drinking.

"In the United States, studies have revealed that in more than 40% of the cases of violent crimes alcohol abuse was involved. This is a jaw-dropping statistic, which definitely proves that alcohol abuse is happening in epidemic proportions and something needs to be done" (AlcoholAddict.imfo).

Pastor Mark Spitesbergen said, "God places the topic of uncleanness as parallel to intoxication. Intoxication with alcohol excites fleshly lust, and brings men under the control of sensuality. It leaves them so transfixed by the earthly, the sensual and the devilish that there is no such thing as wrongdoing in the eyes of the one under its influence."

4. Causes Blackouts "Alcohol can produce detectable impairments in memory after only a few drinks and, as the amount of alcohol increases, so does the degree of impairment. 'Blackouts are much more common among social drinkers than previously surveyed." In a survey of 772 college undergraduates they were asked about their experiences with blackouts , "Have you ever awoken after a night of drinking not able to remember things that you did or places that you went? Of the students who had ever consumed alcohol, 51 percent reported blacking out at some point in their lives. The students reported learning later that they had participated in a wide range of potentially dangerous events they could not remember, vandalism, unprotected sex, and driving" (FAS, National Institute of Health, number 63, October 2004).

Sinning Saints

Bible teachings on abstinence

Do not drink wine nor strong drink, thou, nor thy sons with thee, when ye go into the tabernacle of the congregation, lest ye die: it shall be a statute for ever throughout your generations" (Leviticus 10:8-10).

"He shall separate himself from wine and strong drink, and shall drink no vinegar of wine, or vinegar of strong drink, neither shall he drink any liquor of grapes, nor eat moist grapes, or dried" (Numbers 6:2-4).

"And the drink offering thereof shall be the fourth part of an hin for the one lamb: in the holy place shalt thou cause the strong wine to be poured unto the LORD for a drink offering" (Numbers 28:6-8).

"Ye have not eaten bread, neither have ye drunk wine or strong drink: that ye might know that I am the LORD" (Deuteronomy 29:6).

Sampson's mother told her son, "Now therefore beware, I pray thee, and drink not wine nor strong drink, and eat not any unclean thing" (Judges 13:3).

"She may not eat of any thing that cometh of the vine, neither let her drink wine or strong drink, nor eat any unclean thing: all that I commanded her let her observe" (Judges 13:13-15).

"And Hannah answered and said, No, my lord, I am a woman of a sorrowful spirit: I have drunk neither wine nor strong drink, but have poured out my soul before the LORD" (1 Samuel 1:14-16).

"When Abigail went to Nabal, he was in the house holding a banquet like that of a king. He was in high spirits and very drunk. So she told him nothing until daybreak. Then in the morning, when Nabal was sober, his wife told him all these things, and his heart failed him and he became like a stone. About ten days later, the LORD struck Nabal and he died" (I Samuel 25:36-38).

"Wine is a mocker, strong drink is raging: and whosoever is deceived thereby is not wise" (Proverbs 20:1-3).

Some Bible characters profited by not drinking alcohol

Jonadab's sons were obedient to their father and refused to drink. The Rechabits were warned by Jonadab to drink no wine "But they said, We will drink no wine: for Jonadab the son of Rechab our father commanded us, saying, Ye shall drink no wine, neither ye, nor your sons for ever (Jeremiah 35:6).

Samson was forbidden by his mother to drink strong drink "Then the woman came and told her husband, saying, A man of God came unto me, and his countenance was like the countenance of an angel of God, very terrible: but I asked him not whence he was, neither told he me his name: But he said unto me, Behold, thou shalt conceive, and bear a son; and now drink no wine nor strong drink, neither eat any unclean thing: for the child shall be a Nazarite to God from the womb to the day of his death" (Judges 13:6-7).

"But Daniel purposed in his heart that he would not defile himself with the portion of the king's meat, nor with the wine which he drank: therefore he requested of the prince of the eunuchs that he

Sinning Saints

might not defile himself" (Daniel 1:8).

"For John (the Baptist) came neither eating nor drinking, and they say, 'He has a demon" (Matthew 11:18).

Bible characters who suffered from drinking alcohol:

1. Noah got drunk and exposed himself to his sons (Genesis 9:21).

2 Lot got drunk and committed Incest with his daughters. (Genesis 19:30-36).

3. Nabal was killed by God after a night of drunkenness, "And Abigail came to Nabal; and, behold, he held a feast in his house, like the feast of a king; and Nabal's heart was merry within him, for he was very drunken: wherefore she told him nothing, less or more, until the morning light. But it came to pass in the morning, when the wine was gone out of Nabal, and his wife had told him these things, that his heart died within him, and he became as a stone. And it came to pass about ten days after, that the LORD smote Nabal, that he died" (I Samuel 25:36-37).

4. Elah was murdered by Zimri while he was drunk, "And his servant Zimri, captain of half his chariots, conspired against him, as he was in Tirzah, drinking himself drunk in the house of Arza steward of his house in Tirzah. And Zimri went in and smote him, and killed him, in the twenty and seventh year of Asa king of Judah, and reigned in his stead" (I Kings 16:9-10).

5. Belshazza had his kingdom taken from him by the Assyrians, during a drunken celebration, "Belshazzar the king made a great

Sinning Saints

feast to a thousand of his lords, and drank wine before the thousand. Belshazzar, whiles he tasted the wine, commanded to bring the golden and silver vessels which his father Nebuchadnezzar had taken out of the temple which was in Jerusalem; that the king, and his princes, his wives, and his concubines, might drink therein. Then they brought the golden vessels from the house of God which was at Jerusalem; and the king, and his princes, his wives, and his concubines, drank in them. They drank wine, and praised the gods of gold, and of silver, of brass, of iron, of wood, and of stone. In the same hour came forth fingers of a man's hand, and wrote over against the candlestick upon the plaister of the wall of the king's palace: and the king saw the part of the hand that wrote . Then the king's countenance was changed , and his thoughts troubled him, so that the joints of his loins were loosed, and his knees smote one against another . . . And thou his son, O Belshazzar, hast not humbled thine heart, though thou knewest all this; But hast lifted up thyself against the Lord of heaven; and they have brought the vessels of his house before thee, and thou, and thy lords, thy wives, and thy concubines, have drunk wine in them; and thou hast praised the gods of silver, and gold, of brass, iron, wood, and stone, which see not, nor hear, nor know : and the God in whose hand thy breath is, and whose are all thy ways, hast thou not glorified . . . In that night was Belshazzar the king of the Chaldeans slain (Daniel 5:1-6, 22, 23, 30).

6. The Corinthians – While some were drunk as they took the Lord's Supper some got sick and others died, "For in eating every one taketh before other his own supper: and one is hungry, and another is drunken . . . For he that eateth and drinketh unworthily, eateth and drinketh damnation to himself, not discerning the Lord's body. For this cause many are weak and sickly among you, and many sleep" (I

Sinning Saints

Corinthians 11:21, 29, 30).

Christian excuses for drinking alcohol

Many uninformed church members excuse their drinking by saying, "Jesus drank, Paul drank, and the Bible approves it!" They are ignorant of the fact that the word 'wine' in the Bible to refer to both fermented grape juice and to unfermented grape juice. There is not one verse of scripture saying Jesus drank fermented wine, now served it.

The Bible refers to many kinds of wine, Nehemiah 5:18 says there are "all sorts of wine." The Bible uses the word 'wine' to refer to both fermented and unfermented wine.

Unfermented wine comes forth from the earth, while no alcohol does and it brings gladness to the heart of man. "He causeth the grass to grow for the cattle, and herb for the service of man: that he may bring forth food out of the earth; And wine that maketh glad the heart of man, and oil to make his face to shine, and bread which strengtheneth man's heart" (Psalms 104:14, 15).

The Bible warns against even looking at strong, fermented wine, "Look not thou upon the wine when it is red, when it giveth his colour in the cup, when it moveth itself aright. At the last it biteth like a serpent, and stingeth like an adder" (Proverbs 23:31). You certainly cannot drink strong wine if you cannot even look at it.

Clarks Bible Commentary explains, "Look not thou upon the wine - Let neither the color, the odour, the sparkling, etc., of the wine, when poured out, induce thee to drink of it. However good and pure it may be, it will to thee be a snare, because thou art addicted to it, and hast no self-command."

The Lie of "Drinking Responsibly"

David J. Stewart writes, "Everywhere we go nowadays, people are bombarded with advertisements to "Drink Responsibly"; yet, in spite of the warnings, people are still being maimed and injured by drunk drivers. Little children are still being killed. Who's kidding who? What the lying beer companies will NEVER tell you is that NO AMOUNT of alcohol is safe while driving... "The National Highway Traffic Safety Administration's (NHTSA) position on the relationship between blood alcohol concentration and driving is that driving performance degrades after just one drink."
SOURCE: http://www.nhtsa.dot.gov/people/injury/New-fact-sheet03/Point08BAC.pdf

The Bible prohibits using strong drink

Wine, the strong kind, was forbidden for kings and priests, for those who took the Nazarite vow, It is not for kings, O Lemuel, It is not for kings to drink wine, Nor for princes intoxicating drink; Lest they drink and forget the law, And pervert the justice of all the afflicted. Give strong drink to him who is perishing, And wine to those who are bitter of heart. (Proverbs 31:4-6).

And God pronounced "woe," or judgment upon anyone who served his neighbor alcoholic wine and made him drunk, "Woe unto him that giveth his neighbour drink , that puttest thy bottle to him, and makest him drunken also, that thou mayest look on their nakedness!" (Habakkuk 2:15).

Sinning Saints

The majority of Christians will tell you that they had to ferment grape juice in Biblical times because there was no other way to preserve it. This is a grievous error perpetuated by many boozing pastors and church members.

The Biblical Word Wine and Its Usage

The word "wine" is mentioned 231 times in the King James Bible.

There are 3 Hebrew words that are all translated as "wine" In the Old Testament.

AYIN: Intoxicating, fermented wine (Genesis 9:21).

TIROSH: Fresh grape juice (Proverbs 3:10).

SHAKAR: Intoxicating, intensely alcoholic, strong drink (often referred to other intoxicants than wine) (Numbers 28:7).

The New Testament, translated from Greek, uses the word "wine" for both fermented and unfermented drink.

There are 2 Greek words translated "wine" in the New Testament.

OINOS: Wine (generic) - Matthew 9:17 (fermented), "Neither do men put new wine into old bottles: else the bottles break and the wine runneth out , and the bottles perish : but they put new wine into new bottles, and both are preserved."

GLEUKOS: (unfermented), "Sweet wine, fresh juice "Others mocking said, These men are full of new wine" (Acts 2:13).

The context of the scripture reveals the type of wine. In Proverbs 20:1 says, "Wine is a mocker, strong drink is raging: and whosoever is deceived thereby is not wise." If grape juice is substituted for the word wine, the verse doesn't make sense.

The preposterous 'Alcohol Lie' believed by most Christians

Most Christian have swallowed this monumental lie about alcohol: "In Biblical times they did not have any way to preserve grape juice excepted by fermenting."

Samuele Bacchiocchi, Phd, Andrews University, has done a scholarly study of this subject and uncovered a host of ways they preserved unfermented grape juice in Biblical times. "Here was laid up corn in large quantities, and such as would subsist men for a long time; here was also wine and oil in abundance, with all kinds of pulse and dates heaped up together; all which Eleazar found there, when he and his Sicarii got possession of the fortress by treachery. These fruits were also fresh and full ripe, and not inferior to such fruits newly laid in, although they were little short of a hundred years from the laying in (of) these provisions (by Herod), till the place was taken by the Romans."

Columella, a renowned agriculturalist who lived in the first century A.D. In his treatise On Agriculture and Trees, Columella discusses at enormous length the various methods used to preserve such produce as lettuce, onions, apples, pears, berries, plums, figs, olives, unfermented grape juice and fermented wine. This information should dispel the mistaken notion of the impossibility of preserving

Sinning Saints

grape juice unfermented in Bible times.
1. Seal grapes in honey-water or 'must.'
2. Sealing the cut in the grape vine and placing it in vessels filled with dry chaff. This would preserve the grapes for up to a year.
3. Hanging the grapes by a string from the ceiling preserved them through the winter. Pliny, a Roman scholar and naturalist, describes in his Natural History, other methods used to preserve grapes: "Some grapes will last all through the winter if the clusters are hung by a string from the ceiling" (Pliny, Natural History 14, 3, 16, trans. H. Rackham, The Loeb Classical Library (Cambridge, Massachusetts, 1960).
4. Dipping into boiling pitch and storing them in barley-bran. Just as fruit and vegetables could be preserved in Biblical times, grape juice could also be preserved. The apocryphal Acts and Martyrdom of Matthew, a document which circulated in the second and third centuries of the Christian era, records: "Bring as an offering the holy bread; and, having pressed three clusters from the vine into a cup, communicate with me, as the Lord Jesus showed us how to offer up, when he rose from the dead, on the third day." This is a clear and positive testimony not only of the custom of making grape juice by pressing fresh grapes, and using this unfermented grape juice in the celebration of the Lord's Supper.

Grape juice contains glucose or grape sugar and albumen which contribute to the fermentation process. The albumen contains microscopic organisms, which are the fermenting agents known as ferments or yeast.

The decaying of the albumen in the grape juice affords conditions favorable for the multiplication of yeast germs, which mix with those already present in the air. These release a chemical enzyme capable of breaking down the grape sugar into two forms. One is ethyl alcohol, a colorless liquid that readily mixes with water and remains in solution in the wine. The other is carbon dioxide gas, which appears in tiny bubbles which give the appearance of ebullition.

Early Christians preserved grape juice in four ways:

1. The Preservation of Grape Juice by Boiling.
"By boiling, the water of the grape juice evaporates, yeasts and molds are destroyed, and the sugar content increases, thus inhibiting yeast growth," writes Samuele Bacchiocchi. "This method of preserving grape juice unfermented by carefully boiling it down to a syrup was commonly and successfully used in the ancient world. When desired, the syrup would be drunk diluted with water."

Ancient writers Columella, 40, and Pliny confirm this method. Cyrus Redding, in his History of Modern Wines, states: "On Mount Libanus, at Kesroan, good wines are made, but they are for the most part vino (boiled wines). The wine is preserved in jars." said J. D. Paxton, who witnessed a vintage in Lebanon, also says: "The juice that was extracted when I visited the press was not made into (what is now called) wine, but into what is called dibs."

This method has survived through the centuries in the Near East and Mediterranean countries. This beverage is known as vino cotto (boiled wine) in Italian, vin cuit in French, nardenk in Syriac and dibs in Arabic.

2. The Preservation of Grape Juice through Filtration
Another method by which the fermentation of grape juice can be prevented is by separating the albumen, which is located in the

lining of the skin and the envelope of the seeds of the grape, from the other elements. The albumen contains the fermenting agents.

3. The Preservation of Grape Juice Through Cold Storage.
The fermentation of grape juice can be prevented by keeping it below 40º F (4º Celsius). Nearly all processes of fermentation cease at about 40º F. Fermentation is possible only between about 40º and 80º F(4º and 27º Celsius). "Gibeon's wine cellars were excavated by James Pritchard 1956-62, Gibeon has significant remains especially from the days of the Israelites. He found 63 wine cellars from the 8th-7th centuries BC. These cellars were bottle-shaped and about 6 feet deep and 6 feet in diameter at the bottom. It is estimated that 19,000 gallons of wine could have been stored in 9 gallon jugs in these cellars" (Bibleplace.com, Gibeon).

4. The Preservation of Grape Juice Through Sulphur Fumigation
The fermentation of grape juice can also be prevented by the fumes of sulphur dioxide. The method consists in filling the jars nearly full with fresh unfermented grape juice, then burning sulphur dioxide in the empty portion, and while the sulphur fumes are present, the jars are tightly closed. (For a discussion of the practice of diluting wine among the Romans, see Robert H. Stein, "Wine-Drinking in New Testament Times," Christianity Today (June 20, 1975): 9-11. A more extensive treatment is found in Jimmy L. Albright, "Wine in the Biblical World: Its Economic, Social, and Religious Implications for New Testament Interpretation" (Ph. D. dissertation, Southwestern Baptist Theological Seminary), pp. 176-178. See also Henry J. Van-Lennep, Bible Lands: Their Modern Customs and Manners Illustrative of Scripture (New York, 1875), p. 120; also Edwin Wilbur Rice, Orientalism in Bible Lands, 3rd edition (Philadelphia, 1929), p. 154).

Sinning Saints

The popular belief is "Jesus was not a teetotaler," but a moderate drinker of fermented wine who even 'miraculously' manufactured' a high-quality (alcoholic) wine at Cana and instituted the Last Supper with alcoholic wine." This error has no doubt influenced the drinking habits of millions of Christians around the world more than anything else that the Bible says about drinking.

1. At the Cana wedding, it states 'fruit of the vine,' not wine. In the Luke 22 account of the Passover, the word wine does not appear. John Kitto's Cyclopedia of Biblical Literature refers to the use of unfermented wine at the Passover meal: "The wine used would of course be unfermented, but it is not certain that it was always the fresh expressed juice or 'pure blood of the grape'" (Deuteronomy 32:14).
2. Leaven was forbidden during Passover. During the Passover, which Jesus was celebrating at the time of His Last Supper, the use of any "fermented thing" was prohibited, "Seven days thou shalt eat unleavened bread, and in the seventh day shall be a feast to the LORD. Unleavened bread shall be eaten seven days; and there shall no leavened bread be seen with thee, neither shall there be leaven seen with thee in all thy quarters. And thou shalt shew thy son in that day, saying , This is done because of that which the LORD did unto me when I came forth out of Egypt. (Exodus 13:6-8).

3. Ferment wine cannot symbolize Jesus blood.
Samuele Bacchiocchi, Ph. D., Andrews University, writes, "Jesus used unfermented wine at the Last Supper is the consistency and beauty of the blood symbolism which cannot be fittingly represented by fermented wine. Leaven, we have seen, was used by Christ to represent the corrupt teachings of the Pharisees and is viewed in

Sinning Saints

Scripture as an emblem of sin and corruption. Could Christ have offered His disciples a cup of fermented wine to symbolize His untainted blood shed for the remission of our sins? Could the redeeming and cleansing blood of Christ have been represented aptly by an intoxicating cup which stands in the Scripture for human depravity and divine indignation?"
(For more information on this subject, see: http://www.biblicalperspectives.com/books/wineinthebible/4.htm)

Despite the Bible forbidding "strong" drink, despite the deaths caused by alcoholic drinks, some professed Christians go right ahead and drink with the heathen. They succumb to peer pressure, wanting to be approved by the world more than to be approved by God. Some professed Christians try to escape reality with alcohol instead of changing their reality through the power of God.

Most Christians are controlled by persuasive advertisement. Advertisers would not spend billions of dollars in advertise if it did not make people purchase their product.
(Reference: http://www.cancer.org/Cancer/CancerCauses/DietandPhysicalActivity/alcohol-use-and-cancer).

To preserve your relation with God, your health, and your influenced on your family and friends, repent of drinking alcohol. Go home and pour all the alcohol in your house down the drain.

Judges 13:4 - Now therefore beware, I pray thee, and drink not wine nor strong drink . . ." This is a command of God against drinking 'strong' drink, which can pervert your thinking and even lead to drunkenness.

Sinning Saints

You should not drink, even if you can maintain moderation. There are many who cannot control it and you are influencing them to drink, which may destroy them, "[It is] good neither to eat flesh, nor to drink wine, nor (any thing) whereby thy brother stumbleth, or is offended, or is made weak" (Romans 14:21).

Hosea 4:11 warns, " Whoredom and wine and new wine take away the heart." John Gill's Commentary explains, "Uncleanness and intemperance besot men, deprive them of reason and judgment, and even of common sense, make them downright fools, and so stupid as to do the following things; or they take away the heart from following the Lord, and taking heed to him, and lead to idolatry; or they "occupy" the heart, and fill it up, and cause it to prefer sensual lusts and pleasures to the fear and love of God: their stupidity brought on hereby is exposed in the next verse; though it seems chiefly to respect the priests, who erred in vision through wine and strong drink, and stumbled in judgment (Isaiah 28:7)."

Are you drinking? Has alcohol taken away your heart and left you just a stupid sinner? Stop it today.

Sinning Saints

4
Tattoos: Graffitti on the Temple of God

"The sight of a woman being tattooed live on a church altar accompanied by the sound of a buzzing ink gun provided a startling backdrop to Sunday's evangelical sermon," reports Nick Perry of the Seattle Times. "Your parents' church service this was not. In the need to remain relevant, the Gold Creek Community Church has been hosting a series called 'Permanent Ink' that featured Sunday's live-tattoo finale." When a church features tattooing in a Sunday service, you know it is endorsing the practice.

Mike Tyson was denied entry to the country because of a facial tattoo.

The Las Vegas celebrity had earlier been granted an exception to New Zealand immigration rules to speak at a November charitable event, "Day of the Champions." Tyson's 1992 rape conviction would have usually made him ineligible to enter the country. The government decided to let him in despite his rape conviction. They shut him out of the country, because the tattoo was too much.

Speaking to the APNZ news agency, Tyson said the tattoo on his face was inspired by New Zealand's indigenous Maori culture. In earlier times, many Maori wore elaborate facial tattoos as a sign of their status in their tribe. Some Maori today, who identify strongly with their traditional culture, get similar tattoos.

Sinning Saints

While New Zealand takes a strong stand against such tattoos, America has no such stand.

Current statistics on tattoos by the Source: Pew Research Center for 2012:

- Annual amount of U.S. spending on tattoos $1.65 Billion
- Total percent of Americans (all ages) who have at least one tattoo 14 %
- Percentage of U.S. adults 18 – 25 who have at least one tattoo 36 %
- Percentage of U.S. adults 26 – 40 who have at least one tattoo 40 %
- Total number of Americans that have at least one tattoo 45 million
- Number of tattoo parlors in the U.S. 21,000
- Average cost of a small tattoo $ 45
- Average cost of a large tattoo $150 / hour

Tattooing is not only finding a new popularity among the general population, but many members of Christian churches are participating in the practice. Jesus prayed that the Father would keep Christians from the evils of the world, "I pray not that thou shouldest take them out of the world, but that thou shouldest keep them from the evil" (John 17:15). In complete disregard for Christ's wishes, Christians are turning pagan, joining the worldly.

There are three things wrong with tattoos:

1. Tattoos desecrate the temples of God

Historically temples have been protected from desecration out of reverence for God. The Protection of Holy Places Law of June 27, 1967 shows the evil of desecrating God's temple: "The Holy Places shall be protected from desecration and any other violation and from anything likely to violate the freedom of access of the members of the different religions to the places sacred to them or their feelings with regard to those places."

When Constantine became Roman Emperor he legalized Christianity, and banned tattooing. He believed that the human face was a representation of the image of god and should not be disfigured or defiled. Smearing paint or creating a design upon a temple of God could earn you 7 years in prison. Tattooing is nothing more than writing graffiti on the temple of God, which is the body of a Christian.

Since the day of Pentecost, when the Spirit of God moved into the body of believers, Christians bodies are the temple off God. "What? know ye not that your body is the temple of the Holy Ghost which is in you, which ye have of God, and ye are not your own? For ye are bought with a price: therefore glorify God in your body, and in your spirit, which are God's" (I Corinthians 16:19, 20).

Would you write on a Jewish temple's walls, or draw pictures on then? They call this desecrating the temple of God. Most wouldn't. But many will write of a Christian temple's walls and draw pictures on them. They call this tattooing.

Leviticus 19:8 warns against profaning God's holy things, "He hath profaned the hallowed thing of the Lord: and that soul shall be cut off from among his people." A Christian's body is holy.

2. Tattoos disobey the Bible by making 'cuttings' on the flesh

Sinning Saints

In the time of the Old Testament, pagans practicing tattooing as a way of worshipping their god, responded to this by declaring, "Ye shall not make any cuttings on your flesh for the dead nor print any marks upon you" (Leviticus 19:28).

This established the believers' position on tattooing. The tattoo needle cuts through the skin and allowing the ink to be placed in the flesh. This is in direct disobedience to scripture.

3. Tattooing is preparing mankind for the Anti-Christ

The tattoos are a major step, setting the stage for everyone having a number in their body. "And he causeth all, both small and great, rich and poor , free and bond, to receive a mark in their right hand , or in their foreheads: And that no man might buy or sell , save he that had the mark, or the name of the beast, or the number of his name. Here is wisdom. Let him that hath understanding count the number of the beast: for it is the number of a man; and his number is Six hundred threescore and six" (Revelation 13:16-18).

The Anti-Christ is going to put a number or a name on everyone's body. Putting any kind of number or picture on the body is a drastic, and distasteful act to many people. Tattooing gets people use to marks on their bodies. This will make the anti-Christ's numbers more acceptable.

The dark history of tattoos

The word tattoo comes from the Polynesian word 'ta.' It means

Sinning Saints

hitting something and the Tahitian word 'tatau' meaning 'to mark something'.

In 1991, a five thousand year old tattooed man 'ötzi the ice man' made the headlines of newspapers all over the world when his frozen body was discovered on a mountain between Austria and Italy. He had 57 tattoos, probably done for treatment of arthritis.

Ancient Greek and Rome times

The ancient Greeks decorated their women with tattoos they considered exotic beauty marks.

The Romans adopted tattooing from the Greeks and tattooed slaves and criminals.

The 11th through the 16th Century A.D.

In Peru, tattooed mummies dating to the 11th century were found. The 16th century Spanish accounts of Mayan tattooing in Mexico were thought to be a sign of courage.

In 1519 Cortez and his men were horrified to discover that the natives not only worshipped devils in the form of statues and idols, but had somehow managed to imprint indelible images of these idols on their skin.

The 16th - 19th Century

The arrival of western missionaries in pagan countries forced this unique art form into decline as tattooing was discouraged or

Sinning Saints

forbidden.

Early Jesuit accounts testify to the widespread practice of tattooing among native Americans. These marked outstanding warriors among the Chickasaw, and 'high status' among the Iroquoians. Women's chins were tattooed to indicate marital status and group identity.

In 1891, Samuel O'Reilly invented the electric tattooing machine.

The modern history

Burleson Consulting contributed some of the following modern history.

1850 - 1900 - Tattoos used to be the mainstay of circus freak shows, with people flocking to the circus to see the

stunning tattooed Lady. For over 70 years, tattooed people were exhibited in circuses.

The first permanent tattoo shop in New York city was set up in 1846 and tattooing soon became a tradition among military servicemen

1900 - 1950 - Tattoos in the early 20th century indicated a Sailor or Marine. The tattoos were generally on enlisted men. Few Navy or Marine officers dared to draw on their body. For a long time, tattooing was the preserve of sailors and...criminals!

1950 - 1960 - In the early 1950's, tattoos became popular with the criminal element, largely outlaw bikers, social outcasts and the mentally ill. It was during this time tattoos took on a more sinister reputation.

1960 - 1990 - This was the time of "prison tats" when having a tattoo indicated to some people that you were a tough, ignorant, convicted felon. The ultimate device for gang members are their gang tattoos, getting a permanent mark is a way showing total commitment to a gang. Web tattoos on the elbows represent people killed.

The face and neck tats are almost certain giveaways that the person has been to jail/prison or will be there in a week or two. Looking through police mugshots, you will see many tattoos. The accused are often covered with them. Tattoos became an excellent indicator of bad decision making.

Tattoo's Deadly little Secret

Underneath that cute little tattoo is a extremely serious risk of a deadly blood-borne disease such as AIDS, Hepatitis B, Hepatitis C, tetanus, syphilis, tuberculosis or other blood-borne diseases.

Actress Pamela Anderson contracted the deadly hepatitis C from a simple, small finger "TOMMY" tattoo.

Mayo Clinic warns about the dangers of visiting the tattoo parlors: "Keep in mind that tattoo parlors and piercing venues are not held to the same sterility standards as doctors' offices and hospitals. Few states have hygienic regulations to ensure safe tattooing practices in commercial tattoo parlors, and even fewer monitor and enforce standards."

(Body piercing and tattoos: More than skin deep, Mayo Clinic,

Sinning Saints

www.mayoclinic.com).

"An alarming research study recently published by Dr. Bob Haley and Dr. Paul Fischer at the University of Texas Southwestern Medical School in Dallas uncovered that the "innocent" commercial tattoo may be the number one distributor of hepatitis C. The study was published in the journal Medicine (Haley RW, Fischer RP, Commercial tattooing as a potentially source of hepatitis C infection" (Medicine, March 2000;80:134-151).

Dr. Haley, a former Center for Disease Control (CDC) infection control officer, concludes, "We found that commercially acquired tattoos accounted for more than twice as many hepatitis C infections as injection-drug use. This means it may have been the largest single contributor to the nationwide epidemic of this form of hepatitis."

Dr. Haley concludes, "We found that commercially acquired tattoos accounted for more than twice as many hepatitis C infections as injection-drug use."

According to Dr. Haley's research you are twice as likely to be infected with hepatitis C from getting a tattoo from a tattoo shop than shooting up dope! Each stick carries potential for contamination -- and not just with hepatitis, but also HIV.

"Tattoos can cause chronic skin disorders such as sarcoid, keloid scarring, allergic dermatitis, photosensitivity reactions, psoriasis, and benign or malignant tumors" (www.saintmarys.edu/~health/dyk0010.html).

Some medical centers refuse to perform the critical MRI procedures

Sinning Saints

on people who have tattoos. Tattoo ink contains iron oxide that can cause severe pain if the patient has a tattoo. (www.ezpermanentmakeup.com/IronOxideLetters.htm).

It is crucial for people to get a Hepatitis check shortly after obtaining a tattoo. Hepatitis can exist unnoticed for years while doing serious damage to your body. The sooner you detect Hepatitis the better your chances of survival. If you have a tattoo, get a checkup immediately.

It is not just the needle that has doctors worried. Nineteen people in Rochester, N.Y. developed a nasty skin rash bubbling up on their new tattoo. It was not from the needle. The artist wore sanitary gloves. The ink was contaminated.

The elegant poet, Cowley, wrote these lines:

The adorning thee with so much art,
Is but a barbarous skill;
Tis like the poisoning of a dart,
Too apt before to kill.

Tattoos can be removed, can't they?

People reason, "Well if I don't like the tattoo, I can always have it removed." That is right you can and many of the people who get them do want them removed.

Karen L. Hudson, formerly of About.com, writes, "There are a lot of reasons for possibly wanting a tattoo removed – the positive element of tattoo removal is that you are no longer burdened with a tattoo you seriously regret. If a tattoo is holding you back from getting a job

Sinning Saints

you want or keeps you from attaining goals you have set for yourself, a little pain and scarring may be worth it to you. If you have a gang-related tattoo and are no longer associating yourself with that gang or any gang (good for you!), it would be in your best interests to have it removed. If you have a tattoo that symbolizes hate or prejudice, I hope that you will decide that it is time to let it go. If you are wearing a tattoo of a past love and now you have a new special person in your life, it would be unkind to your new love NOT to get rid of the old tattoo.

According to the American Society of Dermatological surgery, over 50% of everyone receiving a tattoo wants it removed later.

And hear is where the troubles come. The difficulty depends on the color used and whether it was done in a professional tattoo parlor. Removal normally takes between 10 and 15 laser surgery sessions. More complex ones take as many as 25-30 sessions.

When you consider the average single session costs between $4$200 to $800, the removal surgery can cost as much as $2,000 to $40,000. Remember health insurance does not cover tattoo removals.

Plastic Surgeon Tolbert S. Wilkinson, of San Antonio, Texas, who has removed tattoos, explains: "If people only realized how difficult it is to remove a tattoo, understood how costly and how painful tattoo removal is, and recognized that society as a whole still views tattoos as a stigma, maybe they would think seriously before getting one.

"Laser removal costs a minimum of $7,000.00 (national average) per tattoo, and takes at least 10 to 15 treatments, spread out over two or more years. Even with this treatment, the tattoo is still visible"

Sinning Saints

(http://www.heloise.com/tattoo.html).

A former service man writes, "I had a buddy in college who Van Gogh'ed his arms up before the Navy said exposed tattoos were against regulation. The military won't allow any tattoo that's visible in uniform, and considering all the services have short-sleeve uniforms, nothing below the bicep is accepted."

A lady blogger says, "I got a tattoo when I was 18, basically as soon as I was legally able to. It's small, on my hip, easily covered, etc etc. I'm 22 now, and I hate it. It's too small/unnoticeable to warrant getting it removed (can't afford it anyhow), but oh, how I wish I could talk to my younger self and tell her that she is not as edgy as she thinks she is."

Tattoos can keep you from getting jobs

Blogger Michelle Goodman writes this story: "At Sara Champion's previous job as a project engineer for one of the country's top construction firms, visible tattoos for professional staff were against company policy.

"She found this ironic -- not to mention frustrating -- given that her job entailed inspecting job sites filled with tattooed construction workers.

"I was out on site all day, and I wasn't allowed to show any of my tattoos," says the 28-year-old Florida native, whose six large tattoos on her arms and back include a brightly colored sunflower, a marigold and a rendition of a Dia de los Muertos bride and groom on her upper left arm. "Ninety-eight degrees and long sleeves is not so

Sinning Saints

cool when you're in Miami."

These are just some companies that have had no visible tattoo policies at one time:

Wal-Mart

Bank of America

Knott's Berry Farm

Most theme parks (Disney especially)

Delivery Drivers (Fedex and UPS specifically)

Many Retail Organizations (Petsmart, Blockbuster, Kohls, Costco, Old Navy, Gap)

Fast Food (McDonalds, Burger King, KFC, Wendys)

Some corporations maintain a strict policy against visible tattoos, especially companies that must make a favourable impression of the general public.

Burleson Consulting gives these "Business Tips.""Today, a prejudice still exists within corporate America about tattoos, especially since there is a clear and direct correlation between income, education and the percentage of those populations who have tattoos. It is no surprise that tattoos are more popular among the poor and under educated.

Sinning Saints

"Don't kid yourself about the importance of hiding or removing tattoos. If you look at middle management and above in any of the Fortune 50 companies, you will be hard pressed to find any managers that have tattoos, hidden or otherwise.

"You do not have to look hard to find hundreds of corporations which have banned employees with tattoos. San Bernardino County California, bars all employees having visible tattoos, and any piercing in the nose, lip, or tongue that contains jewelry."

Apparently, Scotland Yard doesn't believe a big ol' neck tattoo epitomizes professionalism. The British Police Agency has banned all officers from going on duty with visible tattoos anywhere on their bodies.

A study by Careerbuilders shows that tattoos are a sign of "immaturity, poor judgment and lousy taste:" "Forty-two percent of managers said their opinion of someone would be lowered by that person's visible body art."

Three out of four believe that visible tattoos are unprofessional.

In sum, tattoos send a message to corporate America that you are ignorant, low-income, that you have rotten taste, and worst of all, that you may have a criminal record.

Immediately, either cover your tattoo or cover it if you can.

"Now, to-day, before the heart is hardened by the deceitfulness of sin, cut off, at one stroke, that sinful friendship with the ungodly, and that sinful conformity to the world! Determine this day! Do not delay till to-morrow, lest you delay for ever. For God's sake, for your own

Sinning Saints

soul's sake, fix your resolution now!" (John Wesley, text from the 1872 edition on Dress).

5

The Evils of Immodest Dress

It seems strange to this generation of lukewarm Christians, but the Bible instructs you on rules for how you are to dress. However, this is exactly what it does. Trusting Christ to be your 'Lord' means trusting Him to control your dress.

Dress reveals the heart. If a woman desires to please God she will dress modestly. If she is a self-centered woman who desires, to please herself, she will dress so that other will be jealous of her. If she desires to attract men, she will dress as immodestly as society allows.

Not many religious leaders will criticize a woman's dress because it can get them in serious trouble.

A cleric in Iran's northern Semnan province claims he was beaten up by a woman after telling her to cover up, writes Olga Khazan in the Washington Post. "Hojatoleslam Ali Beheshti, a top religious figure in Shahrmirzad, told a passerby that she was "bad hijab" — a woman who is not fully in compliance with the country's Islamic dress code. "She at first told Beheshti to look the other way, but he repeated his demand. Beheshti told the Iranian Mehr news agency that the woman then pushed him to the ground and began kicking him.

"From that point on, I don't know what happened. I was just feeling the kicks of the woman who was beating me up and insulting me." He said he was hospitalized for three days after the incident, and the

Sinning Saints

region's prosecutor said he was "reviewing the case."

Here in America we are granting more respect for the dress rules of school officials than the rules of God. Teachers are falling victim to the same dress code rules as their students. And, schools are having to set rules for teachers, as well as the students. The number of public schools requiring uniforms has nearly doubled over the past decade to 19%, reports the National Center for Education Statistics.

God instructs women on how to dress to win their husbands to Christ: "Likewise, ye wives, be in subjection to your own husbands; that, if any obey not the word, they also may without the word be won by the conversation of the wives; While they behold your chaste conversation coupled with fear Whose adorning let it not be that outward adorning of plaiting the hair, and of wearing of gold, or of putting on of apparel; But let it be the hidden man of the heart, in that which is not corruptible, even the ornament of a meek and quiet spirit, which is in the sight of God of great price" (I Peter 3:1-4),

Further rules on dress are, "I will therefore that men pray every where, lifting up holy hands, without wrath and doubting.9 In like manner also, that women adorn themselves in modest apparel, with shamefacedness and sobriety; not with broided hair, or gold, or pearls, or costly array;10But (which becometh women professing godliness) with good works.." (I Timothy 2:8-10).

The Matthew Henry Commentary explains this passage as follows: "Here is a charge, that women who profess the Christian religion should be modest, sober, silent, and submissive, as becomes their place. They must be very modest in their apparel, not affecting gaudiness, gaiety, or costliness (you may read the vanity of a

Sinning Saints

person's mind in the gaiety and gaudiness of his habit), because they have better ornaments with which they should adorn themselves, with good works. Note, Good works are the best ornament; these are, in the sight of God, of great price. Those that profess godliness should, in their dress, as well as other things, act as becomes their profession; instead of laying out their money on fine clothes, they must lay it out in works of piety and charity, which are properly called good works.

I Timothy 2:9,10 makes it very clear that Christians are to dress modestly.

There are three basic kinds of 'immodest dress.'

1. 'Peacock' dress that calls attention to yourself.

2. 'High-hat' dress whose expense shows off one's wealth.

3. 'Hooker dress' that arouses sexual desires in others.

Peacock dress
This is dress that calls attention to yourself.
Modesty begins in the heart and is of utmost importance in our walk with God. Modesty was the first issue addressed after the fall, and God clothed Adam and Eve to have fellowship with them (even though no one else was on earth at that time). In I Peter 3:3-6, modesty of the heart and clothing are addressed, "Whose adorning let it not be that outward adorning of plaiting the hair, and of wearing of gold, or of putting on of apparel; But let it be the hidden man of the heart, in that which is not corruptible, even the ornament of a meek and quiet spirit, which is in the sight of God of great price

Sinning Saints

For after this manner in the old time the holy women also, who trusted in God, adorned themselves, being in subjection unto their own husbands: Even as Sara obeyed Abraham, calling him lord: whose daughters ye are, as long as ye do well, and are not afraid with any amazement."

Nancy DeMoss, a leading spokeswoman among Christians, writes, "What is Modesty and why is it so important for the Christian woman to understand, dress & behave modestly? Modesty is the voluntary personal responsibility to behave & dress in such a manner as to not purposely draw attention to oneself, to not think proudly of oneself, and it's a decision to protect from purposeful or unintended' enticement in inappropriate ways & places."

Some excuse immodest dress by saying they can't find modest clothes. To the contrary, it may take time and effort, but modest dress can be obtained. There is even a website devoted to modest clothing-- www.suddenlydarling.com. It provides modest dressing at reasonable prices.

High-hat dress
This is dress that shows off your wealth.

"Let your dress be cheap as well as plain; otherwise you do but trifle with God, and me, and your own souls. I pray, let there be no costly silks among you, how grave soever they may be. Let there be no Quaker-linen, — proverbially so called, for their exquisite fineness," declared John Wesley, the founder of the Methodist Church.

You may say, "I see no harm in expensive dress." Here, is the harm for those whose eyes are not blind:

Sinning Saints

1. It engenders pride in you.

2. The wearing of costly apparel naturally tends to breed the love and desire of being admired and praised.

3. It raises jealousy in those of poorer means.

'Hooker dress'

This is dress designed to arouses sexual desires in others.

Go down and watched the 'women of the night' walk the street. Note how they dress. If you find your clothing to be like the prostitutes, it is a great evil. They are dressed for one purpose, to lure men to pay for their bodies. Would any sincere Christian dare dress as they dress? Such dress is to stimulate the lust of men and persuade them to commit fornication.

"Clothing is to conceal, not to reveal. In the Garden of Eden, God designed clothes to cover our first parents' nakedness, for man could not clothe himself," writes Robert Reed. "Adam and Eve made aprons, but God made coats. There is a difference between the two. As a Christian, we must let God be our designer and not man. The clothing industry is largely controlled by pagans, and they know what sells. Satan has an agenda, and please understand that the fashion world is not neutral. Fashions and styles are to arouse the passions of the flesh. In many cases, packaging is more sensual than raw nudity. We must not allow the world to dictate what we wear. God's Word must be our standard in all areas of Christian life, especially in modesty. Amen."

Sinning Saints

There is a shame in a woman bearing her thigh, "... uncover thy locks, make bare the leg, uncover the thigh, pass over the rivers. Thy nakedness shall be uncovered, yea, thy shame shall be seen : I will take vengeance, and I will not meet thee as a man. (Isaiah 47:2,3). The verse foretold that the Chaldean women would be taken captive, and their captors would force them to cross the river holding up their clothing, exposing their thighs. This reveals their nakedness. God says He would not meet them as a man, with lustful eyes, but He will take vengeance.

Christian youth flock to the beaches in the summer. There, they are allowed to get as near naked as legally possible. This attracts the opposite sex and disregard God's order to dress modestly.

Do not speak of how others dress. The number of those who disobey God does not justify their sin. Scripture has plainly warned you: "Thou shalt not follow the multitude to do evil: neither shalt thou yield in judgment, to the opinion of the most part, to stray from the truth," (Exodus 23:2).

Clearly there must be allowance for those who have never heard these things, those who have never been warned. "And the times of this ignorance God winked at; but now commandeth all men every where to repent," (Acts 17:30).

A young lady came to me after her conversion, and said that she looked in a mirror after dressing for a date. She admitted that everything she was wearing was designed to make her boyfriend lust. She fell under conviction and changed into more modest clothes.

Sinning Saints

6

The Lord's Liars

The Day America Told the Truth, by James Patterson & Peter Kim, reveals that: "91% of Americans lie regularly; 63% men & 52% woman have lied to protect themselves; The 91 percent of those surveyed lie routinely about matters they consider trivial."
All lies, even trivial ones, are an abomination to God: <u>Proverbs 6:17, 18 lists the 7 things that are an abomination to Him. At the top of the list are "a proud look and a lying tongue." God detests lying.</u>
Lying has exploded on the Internet. Ninety percent lies on their 'on line dating profiles.' Men are 6 times worse than women. Women lie about their weight, while men lie about income, education level and, yes, and even being married.relationship status.

Here are some common Internet lies:

"Lying online might have cost you up to $500 in Rhode Island." (John W. Adkisson / Los Angeles Times/ June 27, 2012). You can no longer be prosecuted in Rhode Island for lying about your age, your waistline or your sexual prowess online. Internet lying has become so prevalent, they have legalized it.
Our society may have changed its views on lying. God has not. Lying is still an "abomination" He despises.

And a Louis Harris poll turned up the distressing fact that 65% of high school students would cheat on an important exam. They also lie to their parents: "I finished my home work" is a common one.

Sinning Saints

Flattering Lies

Proverbs 28:26 says, "A lying tongue hates its victims, and a flattering mouth works ruin." Here are a few lies, often called simple flattery:
"You look like you have loss weight."
"I want us to get together some time."
"I can't wait to hear about your trip."
"Yeah, you look great in that dress."
By such flattery you are working ruin on your relationship and your soul.

College students are notorious liars when it comes to exam time. In his latest book, "The Honest Truth About Dishonesty," Dan Ariely says college students' send e-mail lies to their professors reporting the sudden "death" of their grandmothers. It appears, "Grandmothers are ten times more likely to die before a midterm and nineteen more likely to die before finals." You may be just a youth, but your liars are still an abomination that God hates.

Police know what liars people are, regularly hearing such lies as these:
"Officer, if I get a ticket my dad will ground me forever."
"Officer, I have no idea how fast I was going."
"Officer, I needed to get to a restroom fast."
"No, officer, "I did not hit my wife?"

People lie to their family. Thirty-six percent lie about important matters; 75 percent to friends, Security technology firm McAfee's

Sinning Saints

study said over 70% of teens have found ways to avoid parental monitoring on the Internet.

It is amazing how much lying goes on within families. The book "The Day Americas Told the Truth" says, 73 percent lie to siblings, and 69 percent lie to their spouses and 86 percent lie regularly to parents." Are you guilty of saying such things as:
"Honey, I could not have lost the car keys, I never lose anything!"
"This stuff has sentimental value!"
"Don't throw these clothes away, when I lose weight I will need them."
"I Certainly did clean my room."
"I will be home by 11:00 o'clock."

While most Christians wouldn't consider robbing a bank, but they will lie at the drop of a hat. Many donot at all mind misleading others...in the name of good business.
Have you been guilty of telling these lies?
I never got that email.
I'll call you.
Open wide, it won't hurt a bit.
"Your check is in the mail."
Money cheerfully refunded.
We service what we sell.
This offer limited to the first 100 people who call in.
Leave your resume and we'll keep it on file.
Your table will be ready in 5 minutes.
Lying to employer is not consider wrong by employees. In fact 92 per cent of us pad our resumes with falsehoods, according to a study published by Cornell University.

Sinning Saints

Respectable-appearing lawyers, union leaders, governmental officials, and business CEO's perjure themselves on the witness stand, and before the United States Senate. The tobacco industry lied to the face of the government questioners and seemed to have no conscience about it. One who, while testifying under oath, lies about a material matter, has committed perjury, a serious crime that, in the United States, can lead to a punishment of up to five years in prison. How much worse will God's punishment be for lying.
President Clinton, who was honored as the Baptist of the year once, lied to our nation about his sexual relations.

Even Christian Churches lie. Here is one example: "In Oakland, California, the St. Andrew Missionary Baptist Church has been accused of lying about their attendance in order to get taxpayer funding from the local school district. The local Christian private school claimed they had enrolled 195 students with 61 of them labeled as "low income children" in order for the school to receive larger grants" (According to the North County Times),
The Bible has strong words for those that lie in the pulpit: "The ancient and honourable, he is the head; and the prophet that teacheth lies, he is the tail" (Isaiah 9:15).

"Behold, I am against them that prophesy false dreams, saith the Lord, and do tell them, and cause my people to err by their lies . . . I will even forsake you, saith the Lord.And as for the prophet, and the priest, and the people, that shall say, The burden of the Lord, I will even punish that man and and his house" (Jeremiah 23:32-34).
One minister preached this lie and flagrantly printed it on the Internet:: "Practice 7 things and you will have your best life now? You won't get cancer, don't go broke, or lose jobs, if just have enough

Sinning Saints

faith?"

One minister reinforce his sermon on lying by telling the congregation: "Next week I plan to preach about the sin of lying. To help you understand my sermon, I want you all to read Mark 17." The following Sunday, as he prepared to deliver his sermon, the minister asked for a show of hands. He wanted to know how many had read Mark 17. Every hand went up. The minister smiled and said, "Mark has only sixteen chapters. I will now proceed with my sermon on the sin of lying."

Christians are plainly admonished never to lie: "Therefore putting away lying, speak every man truth with his neighbour: for we are members one of another" (Ephesians 4:25).

We are to focus on things that are true and honest, "Finally, brethren, whatsoever things are true, whatsoever things are honest, whatsoever things are just, whatsoever things are pure, whatsoever things are lovely, whatsoever things are of good report; if there be any virtue, and if there be any praise, think on these things: (Philippians 4:8).

Psalms 144:11 says, "Rid me, and deliver me from the hand of strange children, whose mouth speaketh vanity, and their right hand is a right hand of falsehood"

God is holy and He wants us to be holy. A lie could be harmless and innocent but still it's detestable before the Creator.

We lie for different reasons. To escape punishment, to receive benefits and even to get others into trouble. Whatever the reason, "Lying lips are abomination to the LORD: but they that deal truly are

Sinning Saints

his delight" (Proverbs 12:22).

Satan is the father of all liars who has never told the truth: "Ye are of your father the devil, and the lusts of your father ye will do. He was a murderer from the beginning, and abode not in the truth, because" (John 8:44). Satan deceived Eve by Lying to her (Genesis 3:1-13). He attempted to deceive Jesus to disobey the Father's will, by lying to Him. He offered to give Him all the kingdoms of the world And said to him, "All these things will I give you, if you will fall down and worship me" (Matthew 4:9).

Annanias and Sapphria lied to God and were buried together for lying Acts 4:32-37). They promised the price of a piece of land to God. But the profits from this sale were kept in part by the couple, and only a part was laid at the apostles' feet by Ananias. Peter knew instantly that Ananias was lying not to him, but to God and exposed his hypocrisy then and there. Ananias fell down and died (Acts 5:4). When Sapphira showed up, she too lied to Peter and to God, saying that they had donated the entire proceeds of the sale of the land to the church. When her lie had been exposed, she fell down and died at Peter's feet. This was the judgment of the God we some day must bow before.

Men who love lies and practice lying will be barred from heaven: "For without are dogs, and sorcerers, and whoremongers, and murderers, and idolaters, and whosoever loveth and maketh a lie" (Revelation 22:15). Some love to tell them and others love to listen to them. Both are lie lovers who will be barred from heaven."

Lying is a sin that can destroy men in eternity. "But the fearful, and unbelieving, and the abominable, and murderers, and

Sinning Saints

whoremongers, and sorcerers, and idolaters, and all liars, shall have their part in the lake which burneth with fire and brimstone: which is the second death" (Revelation 21:8).

Sinning Saints

7

Hooking up, Shacking up and Fooling Around

Hooking up is a extremely familiar term among college and highschool youth today. It involves two people who do not know each other very, well or at all, getting together for heavy petting or sex. Kathleen Bogle a sociologist at Philadelphia's says that 'hooking up' might lead to dating, later. In days long past dating led to hooking up.

The Internet has a immensely popular classified sections called casual encounters for those looking for no strings attached sex. This leads to bedding down lots of partners without any emotional attachment, and no problems with 'breaking up.' Hooking up is popular because people do not have to share their feelings or make any commitments.

Hooking up has become the most common way to start a relationship. A University study showed that America's sexual revolution has produced a soaring number of out of wedlock births, sexually transmitted diseases, teen pregnancies, and a doubling of the divorce rate.

"Sexting" –Teens Sending Nude Pictures Over the Internet

"One out of every seven Los Angeles high schoolers with a cell phone has sent a sexually-explicit text message or photo," and were also

Sinning Saints

more likely to engage in risky sexual behaviors, according to a study based on a 2011 euters reports.
Girls who sent naked pictures of themselves are more likely, to have had multiple sex partners, use drugs and alcohol and engage in high risk sex.

A study of 1,839 Houston, Texas high schoolers out earlier this summer found that one in four teens had sent a nude photo of themselves through the Internet and were also much more likely to be having unsafe sex.

Pornography: the new drug

An "ABC report also mentioned a teen anti-porn movement called Fight the New Drug. It's a group of young people taking some wise words of warning to high schools and teen groups all across the nation. On their site they mention that 70% of pornography is viewed between 9 a.m. and 5 p.m., when most people are generally at work or school. But here's another tidbit the site shared that struck me: The FBI's statistics show that pornography is found at 80% of the scenes of violent sex crimes or in the homes of the perpetrators. 80 PERCENT! That's 4/5ths of the pie! And that is just what they've found, what about the people who are Internet savvy and know how to cover their tracks?" (Focus on the Family).

Oral sex becoming popular

Karen Weintraub, reported for USA TODAY, Forty-four percent of 15- to 17-year-old boys and 39% of girls of that age engage in some kind of sex with a partner of the opposite gender. More teens have oral sex than vaginal intercourse. The data speaks to changing social mores and the need to educate teens about the risk of contracting a sexually transmitted disease from oral sex, experts say. The study is part of the government's effort to monitor those at risk for sexually transmitted diseases even though they are not yet at risk for pregnancy, if they are only having oral sex.

"The research shows that one in four teens is now having oral sex before vaginal sex — marking the "hierarchical reordering of oral sex in American culture," says Justin Garcia, an evolutionary biologist with the Kinsey Institute at Indiana University. Many sex researchers had believed that oral sex was being used to defer vaginal sex, but that doesn't seem to be the case for most teens today, says Terri Fisher, a professor of psychology at Ohio State University. The only demographic group that postponed vaginal sex until substantially after oral sex were young white girls of educated mothers — perhaps those whose mothers impressed upon them the need to avoid teenage pregnancy, researchers say.

"Fisher says she was surprised by the fact that girls and boys gave and received oral sex equally. Also, they began sexual activity at roughly the same age, with 44% of 15- to 17-year-old boys and 39% opposite-sex partner" (http://usatoday30.usatoday.com/news/health/story/2012-08-16/cdc-oral-sex/5707976...).

Sexting" is linked to sexual promiscuity among teens. "One out of every seven Los Angeles high schoolers with a cell phone has sent a sexually-explicit text message or photo, and were also more likely to engage in risky sexual behaviors, according to a study based on a 2011," Reuters reports.

Teens who sent sexually-explicit texts are seven times more likely to

Sinning Saints

be sexually active than those who said they had never sexted.

Girls who sent naked pictures of themselves are more likely, to have had multiple sex partners, use drugs and alcohol and engage in high risk sex.

A study of 1,839 Houston, Texas high schoolers out earlier this summer found that one in four teens had sent out a naked photo of themselves, through the Internet, were also much more likely to be having risky sex.

Tragically, such conduct is carried on while professing to be followers of the Lord, who commanded, "But fornication, and all uncleanness, or covetousness, let it not be once named among you, as becometh saints" (Ephesians 5:3). Not even once, should it be committed by a Christian.

The church in Thyatira allowed a woman to teach and seduce men in the church, "Notwithstanding I have a few things against thee, because thou sufferest that woman Jezebel, which calleth herself a prophetess, to teach and to seduce my servants to commit fornication, and to eat things sacrificed unto idols" (Revelation 2:20).

The Lord said the church at Pergamos had members practicing fornication, "But I have a few things against thee, because thou hast there them that hold the doctrine of Balaam, who taught Balac to cast a stumblingblock before the children of Israel, to eat things sacrificed unto idols, and to commit fornication" (Revelation 2:14). Our Lord warned them to repent, to stop it, and to do it quickly,, Repent; or else I will come unto thee quickly, and will fight against them with the sword of my mouth.

Sinning Saints

Morning after pills given out at school

The Department of Education is giving morning-after pills and other birth-control drugs to students at 14 New York high schools (The New York Post). These can prevent pregnancy if taken up to 72 hours after unprotected sex.

School nurse offices stocked with the contraceptives can dispense them in an emergency to girls without telling their parents. Parents can opt out, but only two percent has.

A city wide epidemic of teen pregnanciesis causing many to drop out of school. This epidemic comes in spite of the many years these schools have provided condoms.

"We can't give out a Tylenol without a doctor' s order," said a school staffer. "Why should we give out hormonal preparations with far more serious possible side effects, such as blood clots and hypertension?" (The New York Post). For more information: http://www.nypost.com/p/news/local/city_schools_plan_UoW7ke5 l2KRwg43nHzt97H#ixzz27PXzLYDe

Why people fornicate

Sex is an extremely powerful drive that God created to unite two people, "For this cause shall a man leave father and mother, and shall cleave to his wife: and they twain shall be one flesh?" (Matthew 19:5).

Sex is a natural attraction that forms a union between two people

Sinning Saints

and produces off springs. While girls married at 13 or 14 in Bible times, today they are waiting 10 years later to marry. Getting a college degree has become more important that sexual purity. They can put off marriage, but they are not able to put off sex.

God did not make us for the sole purpose of having sex, though some live like it, "Meats for the belly, and the belly for meats: but God shall destroy both it and them. Now the body is not for fornication, but for the Lord; and the Lord for the body" (I Corinthians 6:13).

The temptations to fornicate are everywhere; on television and in movies, music, dancing and risqué clothing styles all encourage sex. Conversations about sex at work, among friends and on talk shows all stimulate a desire for sex. They even advertise automobiles by declaring they are 'sexy.'

What God says about sex

God is for sex more than any of us. He created sex. He created it for married people only. Among the married, sex is fine, "Marriage is honourable in all, and the bed undefiled: but whoremongers and adulterers God will judge" (Hebrews 13:4).

God ordered a one year honeymoon, "When a man hath taken a new wife, he shall not go out to war, neither shall he be charged with any business: but he shall be free at home one year, and shall cheer up his wife which he hath taken" (Deuteronomy 24:5).

The definitions of fornication

"Nevertheless, to avoid fornication, let every man have his own wife,

Sinning Saints

and let every woman have her own husband" (I Corinthians 7:2). Only the unmarried can be fornicators.

Harper's Bible Dictionary defines fornication as: "Any type of illicit sexual activity. Included in the realm of sexual misconduct in the OT are seduction, rape, sodomy, beastiality, certain forms of incest, prostitution (male or female), and homosexual relations. The specific sin of adultery, related to marriage, was considered more serious than the others, however, so that a special set of laws governed it. In the NT, almost any form of sexual misconduct (that is, sexual activity outside the marriage relationship) could be designated as fornication or 'immorality'."

The Definition of adultery

"Webster defines Adultery as: Voluntary sexual intercourse between a married man and someone other than his wife or between a married woman and someone other than her husband" (Webster' Dictionary).

In God's 10 Commandments, He writes, "Thou shalt not commit adultery" (Exodus 20:14).

"And if a woman shall put away her husband, and be married to another, she committeth adultery" (Mark 10:12).

"But as a wife that committeth adultery, which taketh strangers instead of her husband!" (Ezekiel 16:32).

Jesus emphasized, "Ye have heard that it was said by them of old time, Thou shalt not commit adultery(Matthew 5:27, 28)."

Sinning Saints

And he saith unto them, Whosoever shall put away his wife, and marry another, committeth adultery against her (Mark 10:11).

"But I say unto you, That whosoever shall put away his wife, saving for the cause of fornication, causeth her to commit adultery : and whosoever shall marry her that is divorced committeth adultery " (Matthew 5:32).

"But I say unto you, That whosoever looketh on a woman to lust after her hath committed adultery with her already in his heart" (Matthew 5:28).

Leviticus 20 says, "And the man that committeth adultery with another man's wife, even he that committeth adultery with his neighbour's wife, the adulterer and the adulteress shall surely be put to death." The Bible is saying that only the married can commit adultery."

Ross Perot said the reason he fired executives who cheated on their wives was, "If a man's own wife can't trust him why should I?"

Saints have renounced their god, kings have renounce their thrones and spouses have left their lifetime mates, all because of the overwhelming lust for sex.

Sinners excuses for sexual sins

Totally tolerant saints love to justify themselves by quoting this

Sinning Saints

story in which Jesus said to an adulterous woman, "Neither do I condemn thee." They leave out the remainder of Christ's statement, "Go and sin no more."

"And the scribes and Pharisees brought unto him a woman taken in adultery; and when they had set her in the midst, They say unto him, Master, this woman was taken in adultery, in the very act. Now Moses in the law commanded us, that such should be stoned: but what sayest thou? This they said, tempting him, that they might have to accuse him. But Jesus stooped down, and with his finger wrote on the ground, as though he heard them not. So when they continued asking him, he lifted up himself, and said unto them, He that is without sin among you, let him first cast a stone at her. And again he stooped down, and wrote on the ground. And they which heard it, being convicted by their own conscience, went out one by one, beginning at the eldest, even unto the last: and Jesus was left alone, and the woman standing in the midst. When Jesus had lifted up himself, and saw none but the woman, he said unto her, Woman, where are those thine accusers? hath no man condemned thee? She said, No man, Lord. And Jesus said unto her, Neither do I condemn thee: go, and sin no more" (John 8:3-11).

Why didn't Jesus address the issue of homosexuality?

Jesus, both in what he says and what he fails to say, remains on the side of those who reject homosexual practice. "Jesus warned that sexual immorality (the Greek word is plural, porneiai) comes from within and makes people unclean (Mark 7:21). Dr. Gagnon comments, "No first-century Jew could have spoken of porneiai ??? without having in mind the list of forbidden sexual offenses in

Sinning Saints

Leviticus 18 and 20 (incest, adultery, same-sex intercourse, bestiality)."

Weren't some of the "good" people in the Bible homosexual, like David and Jonathan? George Henry wrote that David and Jonathan were homosexual lovers, although he apparently realized that te Biblical evidence of later wives and children speaks against this possibility, so he maintained that their homosexuality was only a passing phase.
(http://www.pleaseconvinceme.com/index/Were_David_and_Jonathan_Homosexual_Lovers)

In homosexual bath houses they often have a statue of David and literature teaching David and Jonathan were homosexual lovers. David had sexual problems, but they were with women, not men. Timothy Dailey reminds us, "To attempt to inject a sexual component into Jonathan and David's relationship is morally wrong; the Hebrew texts are absent of any sexual meaning. One should remember the special place the kisses of greeting and parting have in Middle Eastern culture. . . Again, this is simply the perverted attempt by revisionists to rewrite the Bible to support their views." The Bible warns, " For the time will come when they will not endure sound doctrine; but after their own lusts shall they heap to themselves teachers, having itching ears; And they shall turn away their ears from the truth, and shall be turned unto fables" (II Timothy 4:3-4).

A. Sexual Immorality Destroys the Body

Sex oftens brings on bacyterial STDs (syphilis, gonorrhea, and chlamydia). Also, incurable AIDS Hepatitis, genital herpes. These can destroy your health and even take your life.

As the Bible warns, "And thou mourn at the last, when thy flesh and thy body are consumed, And say, How have I hated instruction, and my heart despised reproof" (Proverbs 5:11-12).

B. Sexual Immorality Destroys the Home

Many do not understand the purpose of sex. Jesus informed us, "And he answered and said unto them, Have ye not read, that he which made them at the beginning made them male and female, and said, For this cause shall a man leave father and mother, and shall cleave to his wife: and they twain shall be one flesh? Wherefore they are no more twain, but one flesh. What therefore God hath joined together, let not man put asunder" (Matthew 19:4-6).

When Sandra Bullock accepted her Golden Blove Award for best actress in 'The Bling Side' she her of her husband Jesse James, "I love you. You are so hot." He certainly was. So hot he had several women on the side while married. This led to their divorce.

C. Sexual Immorality Harms the Potential for Future Marriage

A blogger named 'Guilt' wrote: "As a single girl who desperately wishes to be married – part of the reason I don't believe I will be married is because I have been sexually active in the past, and I believe that other truly good girls will have deserved a good man instead of me. It's hard for me to even consider myself a Christian because of my sexual past – which really isn't extensive, but I still feel like a ruined nothing – worthy of nothing. I probably will not be married, probably will never learn to accept myself and my mistakes,

Sinning Saints

probably will harbor self-hatred until the day I die, But I will always encourage people (not only the girls – mind you) who haven't been active ever, never to do so until they are with their spouse."

D. There is no such thing as "safe sex"

Craig Roberts, an epidemiologist at the University of Wisconsin-Madison's University Health Services department and a member of the American College Health Association, says there's no such thing as totally "safe sex," Roberts says, though oral sex reduces pregnancy risk to zero and HIV risk to almost nothing. He observed that people who perform or receive oral sex are still at risk for herpes, gonorrhea and chlamydia" (Usatoday, 8/15/2012).

E. Sexual Immorality Takes Away Your Freedom

Sex is highly addictive. It quickly turns free people into slaves who cannot cease from sexual sins, "Having eyes full of adultery, and that cannot cease from sin; beguiling unstable souls: an heart they have exercised with covetous practices; cursed children" (II Peter 2:14).

Sexual liberation promised freedom but brought us into bondage, "For when they speak great swelling words of vanity, they allure through the lusts of the flesh, through much wantonness, those that were clean escaped from them who live in error. "While they promise them liberty, they themselves are the servants of corruption: for of whom a man is overcome, of the same is he brought in bondage. (II Peter 2:18, 19).

E. You can die having sex

Sinning Saints

Sex brought death in Biblical days, and it is doing it today, "Neither let us commit fornication, as some of them committed, and fell in one day three and twenty thousand" (I Corinthians 10:8).

"Police charged a 40-year-old Kentucky man with murder, tampering with evidence and abuse of a corpse in the disappearance of a college freshman. The police report says he told police the teen died during sex and he disposed of the body. (Associated Press, Nov 11, 2010)

The Widow of an Atlanta cop, who died during three-way sex, is awarded $3 million" reported the msnbc.com Staff. "A jury in Gwinnett County, Ga., has awarded $3 million to the widow of an Atlanta police officer who died while having three-way sex, finding that his doctor was negligent in not properly diagnosing and treating his heart condition.

"The decision came in a medical malpractice case filed by Sugeidy Martinez, the widow of police officer William Martinez, against Dr. Sreenivasulu Gangasani of Lawrenceville, Ga., and the Cardiovascular Group, where Gangasani is a board-certified cardiologist, according to WXIA-TV.

"According to court documents cited by the television station, William Martinez and a friend were having three-way sex with a woman who was not his wife at a hotel near Atlanta's airport on March 12, 2009. Around 3 a.m., he fell off the bed and became unresponsive. EMTs couldn't revive him. He was pronounced dead less than an hour later at a hospital.

"Nelson Rockefeller died while having sex with his mistress (By Lauren Streicher, MD).

Sinning Saints

"Even the mighty Attila the Hun fell victim to a heart attack that caused his early demise ... on his wedding night no less" (http://www.doctoroz.com/blog/lauren-streicher-md/sex-and-heart-attacks-what-way-...).

"And while people might kid about it being a great way to go, fear of heart attack during sex significantly reduces the amount of sexual activity patients with known heart problems have.

"Other than making your heart go "pitter-patter," what are the cardiac effects of sexual activity?

"Volunteers having sex in a laboratory setting have a significant increase in pulse, blood pressure and respiratory rates. In other words, the heart works harder, pretty much along the same level as with a moderate work out.

"What's really interesting is when similar studies are conducted among married couples in their own bedrooms; heart rates don't increase during sex! In fact, on average, married couples had a LOWER heart rate than recorded during normal daily activities. I actually find it pretty depressing that having sex with your spouse in your own bedroom requires the same amount of exertion as a 2-4 mile per hour stroll on a level surface for a few minutes. That is why studies show that sexual activity is rarely responsible for a myocardial infarction" (http://www.doctoroz.com/blog/lauren-streicher-md/sex-and-heart-attacks-what-way-...).

What was French President Flix Faure doing when he died? One of the greatest legends of people dying curing sex still belongs to the

Sinning Saints

French President Felix Faure, who supposedly died while he was in office, during the act of receiving oral sex from a younger assistant. Actor Matthew McConaughey's mother, Kay McConaughey revealed in a book that her husband, Jack McConaughey died while having sex with her and that is the best way for him to go. The woman also said that she was proud of having a husband like this (http://leisure.ezinemark.com/celebrities-died-during-sexual-intercourse-7736847c...).

"Dea Millerberg testified Monday against her husband Eric, detailing how sex and drugs were involved in the death of 16-year-old Alexis Rasmussen, a North Ogden teen who died while babysitting for the Millerbergs in September of 2011. In a preliminary hearing held Monday, Dea Millerberg testified that she picked up 16-year-old Rasmussen on September 10 to babysit the couple's young children. Sex killed him at 16" (http://www.abc4.com/content/news/top_stories/story/Wife-testifies-of-sex-drug-us...).

Actor David Carradine, found dead and nude in Bangkok, Thailand with this note, "I loved him, but at least he died happy." Two autopsies concluded "accidental asphyxiation" was the lovemaking the culprit in this epic end to a Hollywood legend.

There are a lot of different theories about how Attila the Hun died during sex. One book says he died the night of his honeymoon. Attila liked it rough. So the night he married they were having rough sex, and she ended up breaking his nose and causing a hemorrhage that killed him (http://www.11points.com/Dating-Sex/11_Unbelievably_Insane_Deaths_During_Sex).

Sinning Saints

In 1994, Conservative Prime Minister John Major was lecturing the British public on getting back to decent, family values! It later emerged the same John Major was being unfaithful to his wife at the time of his death!

Sergey Tuganov was a 28-year-old Russian man who found himself in a strange situation. Two women bet him he couldn't sexually satisfy them during a 12-hour threesome. He took the bet... for around $4,300... then he *took a bottle of Viagra and got to work*. After he successfully pulled off the 12-hour orgy, he dropped dead from a heart attack.
1(http://www.11points.com/Dating-sex/11_Unbelievably_Insane_Deaths_During_Sex).

F. Sexual immorality destroys the soul
"But whoso committeth adultery with a woman lacketh understanding: he that doeth it destroyeth his own soul" (Proverbs 6:32).

"Men do not despise a thief, if he steal to satisfy his soul when he is hungry; But if he be found, he shall restore sevenfold; he shall give all the substance of his house. But whoso committeth adultery with a woman lacketh understanding: he that doeth it destroyeth his own soul" (Proverbs 6:30-32).

"Do you not know that the unrighteous will not inherit the kingdom of God? Do not be deceived. Neither FORNICATORS, nor idolaters, nor ADULTERERS, nor homosexuals, nor sodomites" (I Corinthians 6:9-10).

"Now the works of the flesh are manifest, which are these; Adultery, fornication, uncleanness, lasciviousness, Idolatry, witchcraft, hatred, variance, emulations, wrath, strife, seditions, heresies, envyings, murders, drunkenness, revellings, and such like: of the which I tell you before, as I have also told you in time past, that they which do such things shall not inherit the kingdom of God (Galatians 5:19-21).

"Even as Sodom and Gomorrha, and the cities about them in like manner, giving themselves over to fornication, and going after strange flesh, are set forth for an example, suffering the vengeance of eternal fire" (Jude 1:7).

Even the religious leaders were committing the heinous sin of adultery, "I have seen also in the prophets of Jerusalem an horrible thing: they commit adultery, and walk in lies: they strengthen also the hands of evildoers, that none doth return from his wickedness: they are all of them unto me as Sodom, and the inhabitants thereof as Gomorrah" (Jeremiah 23:14).

Promiscuousness curses children and grandchildren, "Flee fornication. Every sin that a man doeth is without the body; but he that committeth fornication sinneth against his own body" (I Corinthians 6:18). Promiscuous sex is a sin against the body because the diseases can spread to you and to your children and grandchildren.

God wants you to tell Him how He can forgive your blatant adultery, "How shall I pardon thee for this? thy children have forsaken me, and sworn by them that are no gods: when I had fed them to the full, they then committed adultery, and assembled themselves by troops in the harlots' houses" (Jeremiah 5:7).

Sinning Saints

It will not be so amusing, when the sweet flames of lust have turned into the sordid flames of hell.

Overcoming sexual temptations

1. Flee temptation when it appears

Albert Barnes said, This (adultery) is a sin where a man is safe only when he flies;

Learn from Joseph. "And it came to pass after these things, that his master's wife cast her eyes upon Joseph; and she said, lie with me. But he refused, and said unto his master's wife, Behold, my master wotteth not what is with me in the house, and he hath committed all that he hath to my hand; There is none greater in this house than I; neither hath he kept back any thing from me but thee, because thou art his wife: how then can I do this great wickedness, and sin against God? And it came to pass, as she spake to Joseph day by day, that he hearkened not unto her, to lie by her, or to be with her. And it came to pass about this time, that Joseph went into the house to do his business; and there was none of the men of the house there within. And she caught him by his garment, saying, Lie with me: and he left his garment in her hand, and fled, and got him out (Genesis 39:7-12).

2. Do not go near places that offer temptation

"My son, attend unto my wisdom, and bow thine ear to my understanding: That thou mayest regard discretion, and that thy lips may keep knowledge. For the lips of a strange woman drop as an honeycomb, and her mouth is smoother than oil: But her end is bitter as wormwood, sharp as a twoedged sword. Her feet go down to death; her steps take hold on hell. Lest thou shouldest ponder the path of life, her ways are moveable, that thou canst not know them." (Proverbs 5:1-6).

"And why wilt thou, my son, be ravished with a strange woman, and embrace the bosom of a stranger? For the ways of man are before the eyes of the LORD, and he pondereth all his goings. His own iniquities shall take the wicked himself, and he shall be holden with the cords of his sins. He shall die without instruction; and in the greatness of his folly he shall go astray" (Proverbs 5:20-23).

"Hearken unto me now therefore, O ye children, and attend to the words of my mouth. Let not thine heart decline to her ways, go not astray in her paths. For she hath cast down many wounded: yea, many strong men have been slain by her. Her house is the way to hell, going down to the chambers of death" (Proverbs 7:24-27).

"If mine heart have been deceived by a woman, or if I have laid wait at my neighbour's door; Then let my wife grind unto another, and let others bow down upon her. For this is an heinous crime; yea, it is an iniquity to be punished by the judges. For it is a fire that consumeth to destruction, and would root out all mine increase" (Job 31:9-12).

3. Go to the cross and declare yourself dead to sin

Just as you trust Jesus to cleanse your past, at the cross, trust that He took your 'old man' to the cross and put him to death, "Mortify therefore your members which are upon the earth; fornication, uncleanness, inordinate affection, evil concupiscence, and covetousness, which is idolatry" (Colossians 3:5).

Sinning Saints

God wants to know why you mock His name, "Will ye steal, murder, and commit adultery, and swear falsely, and burn incense unto Baal, and walk after other gods whom ye know not; And come and stand before me in this house, which is called by my name, and say, We are delivered to do all these abominations?" (Jeremiah 7:9,10).

Sinning Saints

8

Tolerance: the Nation's Great Threat

There is a museum, built by Jews, whose purpose is to teach tolerance. It features the 'intolerant' Naxi party, which was against all but the Arian race, particular against the Jews.

The Museum of Tolerance in Los Angeles has on display a letter written by Adolf Hitler. It called for the elimination of the Jewish people. Written in September 1919, the only document personally signed by Hitler calls for "an anti-Semitism based on reason … [whose]…final aim, however must be the uncompromising removal of the Jews altogether."

Electrosonic created an interactive exhibit of the letter, which is considered one of most notable archival documents in the history of the Second World War.

The magnificent museum's stated goal is to prevent another atrocity like Hitler's Final Solution: "The decision was made to create a museum - but not an ordinary museum of artifacts and documents. As Simon Wiesenthal expressed, it must not only remind us of the past, but remind us to act. This Museum should serve to prevent hatred and genocide from occurring to any group now and in the future.
(http://www.museumoftolerance.com/site/c.tmL6KfNVLtH/b.4866027/k.88E8/Our_History…)

Sinning Saints

It is not only a display of Hitler's plan to destroy the entire Jewish race. It is also documentation of the world's tolerance of this maniac. Hitler could have been stopped long before he soaked the world in blood, if surrounding nations had not been tolerant of him until they were forced to fight for their own survival.

Hitler's intolerance was responsible for the death of 6 million Jews. However, it was the tolerance of Germany's neighbors that allowed Hitler to carry his evil to such heights of wickedness. Nobody wanted to fight Naxism, not until they had no choice but to fight or die.

Hitler's intolerance was a horrible act. But, the tolerance of Germany's neighbors during the rise of the Naxis was also a horrible act. Tolerance of decent people and movements is commendable. But, tolerance of all things, including the evil people and evil organizations is a wicked sin.

The Bible does teach Christians to be tolerant of others, "And he said unto them, Ye know how that it is an unlawful thing for a man that is a Jew to keep company, or come unto one of another nation; but God hath shewed me that I should not call any man common or unclean" (Acts 10:28).

"Tolerance becomes a crime when applied to evil." (Thomas Mann, Death in Venice and Other Tales).

A missionary to India was right on target when he wrote, "Toleration has become so tolerant, that evil is included in that tolerance. We are in danger of becoming 'moral cows' in our plump comfortableness."

Sinning Saints

Dorothy L. Sayers captured the enormity of those who tolerate everything, "In the world it is called Tolerance, but in hell it is called Despair...the sin that believes in nothing, cares for nothing, seeks to know nothing, interferes with nothing, enjoys nothing, hates nothing, finds purpose in nothing, lives for nothing, and remains alive because there is nothing for which it will die."

Speaking of the man who is tolerant of evil, G.K. Chesterton said, "Tolerance is the virtue of a man without convictions."

Tolerance has risen to become a dominant virtue in today's world. It means particularly moral issues, and religious issues are to be accepted by all. America is susceptible to such ideas because it has freedom of speech, religion and the freedom of dissent.

We live in a country that teaches its children that there are no absolutes—no absolute morals, no absolute right and wrong. Schools teach that everyone's values, everyone's beliefs, everyone's lifestyles, and everyone's truth claims are equal. Tragically, even the church has begun teaching tolerance. Some are participating in prayer meetings with Jews and Muslims. All faiths are equal in the eyes of many. It is tolerance at its most extreme.

"If we continue to teach about tolerance and intolerance instead of good and evil, we will end up with tolerance of evil," wrote Dennis Prager. And, this is exactly what has happened in much of Western Civilization.

Schools are promoting an extreme tolerance. A typical article in the magazine "Teaching Tolerance " says, "(This) Magazine takes an in-depth look at how educators can use social media to teach social

Sinning Saints

justice. It also explores the human side of the complex immigration debate and suggests ways for educators to defuse the issue in class discussions. Other topics include combating anti-Muslim bias, improving diversity in STEM classes, teaching about human trafficking and changing attitudes about bullies. (http://www.tolerance.org/magazine/number-39-spring-2011).

In the new educational strategy entitled Quality Performance Accreditation (OBE), the Kansas State Board of Education in 1992 adopted ten "clearly defined outcomes that all students must demonstrate when they exit." One of those was written as follows: "All students are tolerant of individual differences and work together without prejudice." That is tolerance with no exception

However, in reality it is our culture and its world system that is intolerant to Christians who believe that the Word of God is infallible, trustworthy, and true, bias, or discrimination.

Some churches are promoting an extreme tolerance

One minister proclaimed it straight forward: "In our post-modern world, 'tolerance' is the one virtue that is esteemed above all others." It may soon become the only virtue our society will accept. Traditional virtues such as humility, chastity and temperance have long fallen out of public favor, and in some circles, are openly ridiculed. Acts once universally labeled "immoral" and "ungodly" are now celebrated under the guise of "tolerance."

In a sermon entitled "Teach us Tolerance and Love" a minister said, "I attended a "laboratory of tolerance" some months ago when I had the privilege of participating in the Parliament of the World's

Sinning Saints

Religions. There, I conversed with good men and women representing many religious groups. Again I sensed the advantages of ethnic and cultural diversity and reflected once more on the importance of religious freedom and tolerance."

The strongest advocates of tolerance actually only want us to be tolerant of what they like. The same people who are extremely intolerant of things like rape, child abuse and environmental pollution. It is not a crime to be intolerant. Tolerance is neither good or bad. Tolerance of bad things is evil and intolerance of certain things is a great good. All people are intolerant, of the things they do not like.

Christians are castigated as "hate mongers" because the Bible condemns sins enjoyed by the masses. "Woe unto them that call evil good, and good evil; that put darkness for light, and light for darkness; that put bitter for sweet, and sweet for bitter!" (Isaiah 5:20).

Who is tolerant of such evils as the idea that blacks are inferior to whites? Who is tolerant of cannibalism? Who is tolerant of thieves? Who is tolerant of murderers?

Americans are taught to tolerate everyone except the Christian. And, why is there no tolerance of us? Charisma magazine gave this answer:

"President Harry Truman during his 1948 presidential election campaign. One of his supporters yelled out to him, "Give 'em hell, Harry!" Truman responded, "I don't give them hell. I just tell the truth about them and they think it's hell. That is precisely the reason

Sinning Saints

why there is a war on Christians waged by members of the secular media. Christians speak the truth about God's best for humanity as it applies to morality, laws and governing principles, but the secular media views these truths as hell. Truth always feels like hell to those who reject, deny or hate the truth."

'The mistaken idea that tolerance is always a virtue and intolerance always a vice is corrupting the very heart of our society" declared Gary Ray Branscome. "In the name of tolerance every evil is exalted and proudly defended, while all those who resist and condemn evil are smeared and demonized as hate mongers and bigots. What are such smear tactics other than intolerance and bigotry on the part of those who claim to be tolerant? Like all who are self-righteous, the dogmatic zealots of tolerance often reveal themselves to be extremely intolerant of anything they disapprove of, yet they refuse to see any fault in themselves."

It is becoming like it was in the Roman empire. The ancient Romans demonized the Christians of their day and persecuting them unmercifully because they were intolerant of the Roman idols. Their Pantheon was built to honor all gods and would have gladly have included Jesus among their many gods. But Christians believe Jesus is the only true God. They died for not being tolerant of those idols"

The Bible denounces tolerance of evil

When the children of Israel first entered the land of Cannan, God ordered the people of that land destroyed because they were tolerant of human sacrifice (abortion), immorality, and false religion (Deuteronomy 20:17).

Sinning Saints

God forbid any tolerance of professed Christians living immoral lives: "But now I have written unto you not to keep company, if any man that is called a brother be a fornicator, or covetous, or an idolater, or a railer, or a drunkard, or an extortioner; with such an one no not to eat" (I Corinthians 5:11).

"I know thy works, and thy labour, and thy patience, and how thou canst not bear them which are evil: and thou hast tried them which say they are apostles, and are not, and hast found them liars" (Revelation 2:2).

Psalm 1:1-6 Blessed is the man who walks not in the counsel of the wicked, nor stands in the way of sinners, nor sits in the seat of scoffers:"

"Now I beseech you, brethren, mark them which cause divisions and offences contrary to the doctrine which ye have learned; and avoid them" (Romans 16:17).

Eli rebuked his sons but tolerated their sin and lost his ministry. "Now Eli was very old , and heard all that his sons did unto all Israel; and how they lay with the women that assembled at the door of the tabernacle of the congregation. And he said unto them, Why do ye such things? for I hear of your evil dealings by all this people. Nay, my sons; for it is no good report that I hear: ye make the LORD'S people to transgress "Give not that which is holy unto the dogs, neither cast ye your pearls before swine, lest they trample them under their feet, and turn again and rend you" (II Samuel 2:22-24).

Eli told his sons not to sin but tolerated them.This brought God's judgment. "For I have told him that I will judge his house for ever for

Sinning Saints

the iniquity which he knoweth ; because his sons made themselves vile, and he restrained them not" (I Samuel 3:13).

Jesus did not tolerate the sinful money changers. "And the Jews' passover was at hand, and Jesus went up to Jerusalem, And found in the temple those that sold oxen and sheep and doves, and the changers of money sitting: And when he had made a scourge of small cords, he drove them all out of the temple, and the sheep, and the oxen; and poured out the changers' money, and overthrew the tables; And said unto them that sold doves, Take these things hence; make not my Father's house an house of merchandise. And his disciples remembered that it was written, The zeal of thine house hath eaten me up" (John 2:13-17).

The Bible denounces tolerance of wicked people

Some time later, God's wrath was poured out on the children of Benjamin because they had become tolerant of evil (Judges 19:22-30 and 20:1-48). The Apostle Paul rebuked the congregation at Corinth because it tolerated fornication, and he pronounced a curse on those who pervert the gospel (1Corinthians 5:1-13, Galatians 1:6-9). Therefore, it should be perfectly clear that we are not to tolerate sin, but are rather to condemn or rebuke it.

The Bible tells us that God not only condemned Sodom and Gomorra for tolerating evil, but also condemned Babylon, Gibeah, Egypt, and other nations for the same reason (Judges 19:15-30, Genesis 19). Therefore, tolerating evil is not a virtue, no matter how hard Satan wants you to believe that it is.

The Bible teaches tolerance regarding every thing that is not evil.

Sinning Saints

Scripture's Golden Rule says, "Therefore all things whatsoever ye would that men should do to you, do ye even so to them: for this is the law and the prophets" (Matthew 7:12).

We are not to even eat with immoral, greedy, idolaters, revilers, drunkards, or swindlers who are in the church.

Jesus commended Christians who were intolerant of false teachers. In Revelation 2:2 He declares, "I know your works, your toil and your patient endurance, and how you cannot bear with those who are evil, but have tested those who call themselves apostles and are not, and found them to be false."

We then, as workers together with him, beseech you also that ye receive not the grace of God in vain. (For he saith, I have heard thee in a time accepted, and in the day of salvation have I succoured thee: behold, now is the accepted time; behold, now is the day of salvation.)

"Be ye not unequally yoked together with unbelievers: for what fellowship hath righteousness with unrighteousness? and what communion hath light with darkness? And what concord hath Christ with Belial? or what part hath he that believeth with an infidel? And what agreement hath the temple of God with idols? for ye are the temple of the living God; as God hath said, I will dwell in them, and walk in them; and I will be their God, and they shall be my people. Wherefore come out from among them, and be ye separate, saith the Lord, and touch not the unclean thing; and I will receive you, And will be a Father unto you, and ye shall be my sons and daughters, saith the Lord Almighty" (II Corinthians 6:14-18).

Sinning Saints

Excuses for tolerance of evil

Advocates of total tolerance often quote the scripture, "Neither do I condemn you" (John 8:11). If you remember, the context is with the woman taken in adultery, in the very act of sexual sin. However, few people today want to say all that Jesus said and quote the last part of the verse, "Go and sin no more." This is not a suggestion. Our Lord Jesus said go and stop sinning! Yes, He did not condemn her but, He also said go and stop your sinning. The Lord Jesus took the woman where she was but, she didn't stay there. It is true the woman was a harlot but not after she met our Lord. Paul says in I Corinthians 6:11, "And such were some of you." He goes on to say, "But you were washed." He identifies homosexuals and adulterers and thieves in the church at Corinth but, he reveals that they did not stay that way.

These advocates of tolerance have a favorite verse. It is Matt. 7:1; "Judge not, that you be not judged." They are willfully ignorant of this verse, "But he that is spiritual judgeth all things" (I Corinthians 2:15).

To understand the two verses it is necessary to learn the two meanings of the word. It can mean, according to Webster's dictionary, "to pass judgment on." Second, it can be used, again from Webster, "to criticize or censure...to think or suppose, as in "If ye have judged me to be faithful to the Lord" (Acts 26:15). The first, which Christ forbid, means to say, "That drunk ought to go to hell." The second use of the word means to say that man's drunkenness is wrong. This is a righteous judgment encouraged by the Bible. To say that drunkard ought to be put into hell is wrong. Jesus' condemnation of judging was against hypocritical one.

Peter reminds us to "be of sound judgment" since "the end of all

Sinning Saints

things is at hand," (1 Peter 4:7).

"Do ye not know that the saints shall judge the world? and if the world shall be judged by you, are ye unworthy to judge the smallest matters? Know ye not that we shall judge angels? how much more things that pertain to this life?" (I Corinthians 6:2-3).

Judge not according to the appearance, but judge righteous judgment" (John 7:24). Jesus tells us to judge, but to do so righteously. We are to judge 'behavior' by the Bible, to judge the deed, not the doer.

Paul commanded Christians to judge those in the church and to put those in wickedness out of the congregation. "But now I have written unto you not to keep company, if any man that is called a brother be a fornicator, or covetous, or an idolater, or a railer, or a drunkard, or an extortioner; with such an one no not to eat. For what have I to do to judge them also that are without? do not ye judge them that are within? But them that are without God judgeth. Therefore put away from among yourselves that wicked person" I wrote unto you in an epistle not to company with fornicators: Yet not altogether with the fornicators of this world, or with the covetous, or extortioners, or with idolaters; for then must ye needs go out of the world. But now I have written unto you not to keep company, if any man that is called a brother be a fornicator, or covetous, or an idolater, or a railer, or a drunkard, or an extortioner; with such an one no not to eat. For what have I to do to judge them also that are without? do not ye judge them that are within? But them that are without God judgeth. Therefore put away from among yourselves that wicked person. 1 Corinthians 5:9-13).

Sinning Saints

Tolerance of Abortion

Despite what the Bible says, masses of Americans blatantly approve of murdering an unborn child. The Bible says that causing a woman's baby to depart from her, should be punished. "If men strive, and hurt a woman with child, so that her fruit depart from her, and yet no mischief follow: he shall be surely punished, according as the woman's husband will lay upon him; and he shall pay as the judges determine" John Gill's commentary explains:

Exodus 21:22 is a Bible passage strongly condemning abortion.

If men strive
quarrel and fight with each other
and hurt a woman with child;
one of the men strikes a woman who is expecting
so that her fruit depart from her;
or, "her children go forth", out of her womb, as a result of the blow
she has a miscarriage or a premature birth
and yet no mischief follow:
no mischief indicates neither the woman or her baby die or are injured
he shall surely be punished;
that is, be fined or mulcted for striking the woman, and hastening the childbirth:
according as the woman's husband will lay upon him; and he shall pay as the judges determine;
the husband might propose what fine should be paid, and if the judge agrees, it is settled.

Sinning Saints

Tolerance of homosexuality

In Lebanon, there is no tolerance of homosexuality. They are conducting "anal tests," to determine whether the patient has been involved in anal intercourse, which is illegal in that country.

A Florida pastor has come forward to argue that it is not Christian, nor healthy, to go seeking out the sin of others. "To go around and search out people who may be considered offenders is not a Christian or a healthy thing to do," Florida Pastor Jack Hakimian of Impact Miami Church told The Christian Post.
Hakimian recently attended a "GLBT Inclusion" forum in North Miami. It was to "present a Christian perspective of tolerance [and] love," and to find better ways for Christian and homosexual communities to peacefully and lovingly exist in society.

The president of the Alliance Defense Fund, an organization fighting in partnership with the Family Research Council, said, "Homosexual behavior and religious freedom. These two are incompatible. The goal of the radical homosexual activists is to make sure that no church can say that homosexual behavior is sinful.
"[God says homosexuality is a "grievous sin," "And the LORD said, Because the cry of Sodom and Gomorrah is great, and because their sin is very grievous" (Genesis 18:20); a "wicked thing," "And said, I pray you, brethren, do not so wickedly" (Genesis 19:7); "an abomination" (Leviticus 18:22); one act of homosexuality meant "they must be put to death; their blood will be on their own heads" "If a man also lie with mankind, as he lieth with a woman, both of them have committed an abomination: they shall surely be put to death; their blood shall be upon them" (Leviticus 20:13).

Sinning Saints

Homosexuality is caused by "shameful lusts," is "unnatural," an "indecent act," and "perversion."

"For this cause God gave them up unto vile affections: for even their women did change the natural use into that which is against nature: And likewise also the men, leaving the natural use of the woman, burned in their lust one toward another; men with men working that which is unseemly, and receiving in themselves that recompence of their error which was meet. And even as they did not like to retain God in their knowledge, God gave them over to a reprobate mind, to do those things which are not convenient; Being filled with all unrighteousness, fornication, wickedness, covetousness, maliciousness; full of envy, murder, debate, deceit, malignity; whisperers" (Romans 1:26-29).

Those who practice homosexuality will not "inherit the kingdom of God" (1 Corinthians 6:9-10).

"If a man also lie with mankind, as he lieth with a woman, both of them have committed an abomination: they shall surely be put to death; their blood shall be upon them" (Leviticus 20:13).

"Thou shalt not lie with mankind, as with womankind: it is abomination" (Leviticus 18:22).

"No Israelite man or woman is to become a shrine prostitute." (Deuteronomy 23:17).

"Know ye not that the unrighteous shall not inherit the kingdom of God? Be not deceived: neither fornicators, nor idolaters, nor adulterers, nor effeminate, nor abusers of themselves with mankind,

Sinning Saints

Nor thieves, nor covetous, nor drunkards, nor revilers, nor extortioners, shall inherit the kingdom of God" (I Corinthians 6:9-10).

"For whoremongers, for them that defile themselves with mankind, for menstealers, for liars, for perjured persons, and if there be any This refers to homosexual and child molesters.

"And the LORD said, Because the cry of Sodom and Gomorrah is great, and because their sin is very grievous; I will go down now, and see whether they have done altogether according to the cry of it, which is come unto me; and if not, I will know ... Then the LORD rained upon Sodom and upon Gomorrah brimstone and fire from the LORD out of heaven" (Genesis 18:20-21; 19:24).

The testimony of the Bible's condemnation of homosexuality is simply overwhelming.

Dr. Robert Gagnon also tells us, "Quite appropriately, an absurd exchange of God for idols leads to an absurd exchange of heterosexual intercourse for homosexual intercourse. A dishonoring of God leads to a mutual dishonoring of selves. A failure to see fit to acknowledge God leads to an unfit mind and debased conduct." The Apostle Paul is crystal clear; same-sex intercourse is sinful, shameful and is itself part of God's sentence of judgment upon the guilty.

Tolerance of laziness

Laziness has become the chief characteristic of Western Christianity, displacing the unbelief.

Sinning Saints

The church has not spoken out on the sin of laziness and the result has been a generation that thinks it is 'entitled' to everything they want, without having to work for it. This invariably turns a nation against capitalism and for socialism.

The Bible is clear about laziness:
The lazy man can always find an excuse not to leave the house and go to work. "The slothful man saith, There is a lion without, I shall be slain in the streets" (Proverbs 22:13).

The lazy man doesn't even get out of bed to go to work. "As the door turneth upon his hinges, so doth the slothful upon his bed" (Proverbs 26:14).

Worse still he is too lazy to lift his hand to put food in his mouth! "The slothful hideth his hand in his bosom; it grieveth him to bring it again to his mouth" (Proverbs 26:15).

A man who is too lazy to work and provide for his family "hath denied the faith, and is worse than an infidel" (1 Timothy 5:8).

Know the true value of time; snatch, seize, and enjoy every moment of it. No idleness, no laziness, no procrastination: never put off till tomorrow what you can do today," said Lord Chesterfield.

Tolerant of the loss of religious freedom

It began 50 years ago when prayer was ordered out of schools.

On August 1, millions of Americans lose their freedom of religion "These are strong words, yes," writes Christen Varley. " To those of us whose faith is an integral part of our daily lives, they are appropriate... On August 1st, businesses and organizations must begin renewing health insurance benefits that include, free of charge,

Sinning Saints

contraceptives, abortion-inducing drugs and sterilization... Employers with religious and moral objections to the mandate must choose between two poison pills: comply and desert your faith, or resist and be subject to crippling fines." (Christen Varley is executive director of Conscience Cause)

"North Dakota voters rejected a controversial measure, in 2012,that would have added an amendment to the state constitution prohibiting the government from putting a "burden [on] a person's or religious organization's religious liberty," writes Morgan Feddes "The amendment was defeated by approximately two-thirds, 64 percent to 36 percent. Known as the Religious Liberty Restoration amendment, supporters of Measure 3 argued it would prevent attacks on religious freedom."

Tolerance of false teachers of the Bible

Do you know how intolerant some of the people are who constantly talk about tolerance? You must be tolerant of all the "great religions." In fact, you must be tolerant of everybody except those who strongly believe that Jesus is the only Savior. You will be called intolerant, bigoted or worse. Intolerance of other religions is what got Jesus nailed to a cross.

"For there are certain men crept in unawares, who were before of old ordained to this condemnation, ungodly men, turning the grace of our God into lasciviousness, and denying the only Lord God, and our Lord Jesus Christ" (Jude 1:4). There ungodly men teaching that grace is a license to sin. These men are denying the teachings of our Lord and leading multitudes astray.

"Can two walk together, except they be agreed?" (Amos 3:3).

Carlton Pearson, former Pentecostal bishop, believes, "the Gospel of Inclusion is consistent with the words of Jesus and other apostolic

Sinning Saints

writings" (p. 12, New York: Atria, 2006). He certainly is not speaking of the same Jesus revealed in the Bible.

Any man teaching contrary to the Bible, should not even be allowed into your house. II John 1:10-11 commands, " If anyone comes to you and does not bring this teaching, do not receive him into your house or give him any greeting, for whoever greets him takes part in his wicked works."

Anyone teaching a doctrine contrary to what our Lord taught should be labeled as someone stirring up controversy and out to main a financial gain. "If any man teach otherwise, and consent not to wholesome words, even the words of our Lord Jesus Christ, and to the doctrine which is according to godliness; He is proud, knowing nothing, but doting about questions and strifes of words, whereof cometh envy, strife, railings, evil surmisings, Perverse disputings of men of corrupt minds, and destitute of the truth, supposing that gain is godliness: from such withdraw thyself" (1Timothy 6:3-5).

In Revelation 2:20-23 Jesus rebuked a church for tolerating an immoral woman to teach. "But I have this against you, that you tolerate that woman Jezebel, who calls herself a prophetess and is teaching and seducing my servants to practice sexual immorality and to eat food sacrificed to idols."

E.L. Bynum said, "Those who are faithful in exposing error according to the Bible are now being widely denounced, and are accused of being unloving and unkind."

Jesus said, "Judge not, that ye be not judged" (Matthew 7: 1). But, in John's Gospel judging is futher explained. "Judge not according to the appearance, but judge righteous judgment" (John 7:24). Here, our Lord commands that we are to "judge righteous judgment, "which is judgment based upon the Word of God. If judgment is made upon any other basis, other than the Word of God, it is a violation of Matthew 7: 1. Webster's Dictionary says that a judge is "one who

Sinning Saints

declares the law. " The faithful Christian must discern or judge on the basis of God's inspired Word, the Bible.

Standing face to face with these false teachers, Jesus Christ the Son of God, called them "hypocrites", "blind guides, " "blind, " "whited sepulchres, " "serpents, " and "ye generation of vipers" (Matt. 23:23-34). Yet, we are told today that we are to fellowship with men whose doctrines are just as unscriptural as those of the Pharisees. Some who say they are Bible believing Christians, insist on working with Roman Catholics and other assorted heretics. According to many, we are not supposed to rebuke them for their false teachings.

"Ye shall know them by their fruits. Do men gather grapes of thorns, or figs of thistles? Even so every good tree bringeth forth good fruit, but a corrupt tree bringeth forth evil fruit" (vs. 16,17). Did the Lord mean that we could not judge the tree (person), by the fruit of their life and doctrine? Certainly not, for you cannot know without judging. All judgment should be on the basis of Bible teaching, not according to whims or prejudices.
(http://www.av1611.org/crock/judbynum.html).

Scripture teaches us, "If any man teach otherwise, and consent not to wholesome words, even the words of our Lord Jesus Christ, and to the doctrine which is according to godliness; He is proud, knowing nothing, but doting about questions and strifes of words, whereof cometh envy, strife, railings, evil surmisings, Perverse disputings of men of corrupt minds, and destitute of the truth, supposing that gain is godliness: from such withdraw thyself. (I Timothy 6:3-5).

Today some pastors use obscene language and tell jokes that are sexual in nature. They do this despite God's clear command: "Neither filthiness, nor foolish talking, nor jesting, which are not convenient: but rather giving of thanks" (Ephesians 5:4).

The pastor of a huge church in Seattle Washington is said to use profanity in the pulpit!

Sinning Saints

Paul "judged" a sexually immoral church member. He told the Church at Corinth that they were to "judge" those that were within. "I wrote unto you in an epistle not to company with fornicators: Yet not altogether with the fornicators of this world, or with the covetous, or extortioners, or with idolaters; for then must ye needs go out of the world. But now I have written unto you not to keep company, if any man that is called a brother be a fornicator, or covetous, or an idolater, or a railer, or a drunkard, or an extortioner; with such an one no not to eat. For what have I to do to judge them also that are without? do not ye judge them that are within? But them that are without God judgeth. Therefore put away from among yourselves that wicked person" (I Corinthians 5:9-14).

There is a conspiracy of silence among many Bible believers. Wolves in sheep's clothing are ravaging the flock,and no one says a word!

11John the Baptist called the Pharisees and Sadducees (the religious leaders of his day) "a generation of Vipers" (snakes) (Matt. 3:7). Today, he would be accused of being intolerant, unloving, unkind, and unchristian.

Jesus said to the religious Pharisees, "O generation of vipers, how can ye, being evil, speak good things? for out of the abundance of the heart the mouth speaketh" (Matthew 12:34). To many evangelicals and some fundamentalists, this would be unacceptable language today, but it is biblical language and it came from the mouth of the Son of God.

We are to TRY prophets. "Beloved, believe not every spirit, but try the spirits, whether they be of God; because many false prophets are gone out into the world" (I John 4: 1). "To the law and to the testimony: if they speak not according to this word, it is because there is no light in them" (Isa. 8:20). Every preacher and every teacherwill be judged by the Word of God. The church at Ephesus was commended because they had "tried them which say they are

Sinning Saints

apostles, and are not, and hast found them liars " (Rev. 2:2). The church at Pergamos was rebuked because they tolerated those that held "the doctrine of Balaam, " and "the doctrine of the Nicolaitanes," which God hated (Rev. 2:14,15).

We are to MARK false prophets and AVOID them. "Now I beseech you, brethren, mark them which cause divisions and offences contrary to the doctrine which ye have learned; and avoid them " (Rom. 16:17). They must be judged by the Word of God.

We are to REBUKE false prophets. "Wherefore rebuke them sharply, that they may be sound in the faith " (Titus 1: 13). This was written to Titus, because there were teachers going from house to house and subverting them with false doctrine (v. 10-16). The faithful servant of the Lord is to be "Holding fast the faithful word as he hath been taught, that he may be able by sound doctrine both to exhort and to convince the gainsayers " (Titus 1:9).

We are to WITHDRAW from false prophets. "Now we command you, brethren, in the name of the Lord Jesus Christ, that ye withdraw yourselves from every brother that walketh disorderly, and not after the tradition which ye received of us " (II Thessalonians 3:6). We must admonish them"if any man obey not our word by this epistle, note that man and have no company with him, that he may be ashamed. Yet, count him not as an enemy, but admonish him as a brother" (II Thessalonians 3:14-15). Paul admonished Timothy to "withdraw thyself " from those who "consent not to wholesome words ... and to the doctrine which is according to godliness" (I Timothy 6:3-5).

We are NOT to RECEIVE false prophets into our house. " "If there come any unto you, and bring not this doctrine, receive him not into your house, neither bid him God speed : For he that biddeth him God speed is partaker of his evil deeds" (II John 1:10, 11). By television, and radio, false prophets are brought into the homes of masses of Christians today. Those who do not turn the false teachers off are

Sinning Saints

disregarding the teaching of scripture.

The 'total tolerance' crowd would like to see all religions worship together and simply ignore false doctrine in the name of 'love.' But they totally disregard the Word of God when they do.

William MacDonald states: "It is an ungodly tolerance that has allowed so many pulpits in America to be filled with 'false apostles and deceitful workers, transforming themselves into apostles of Christ'."

J Sidlow Baxter writes "Such are the people who today, with sickly kindness, will tolerate teachers of errors in our pulpits because they are such smooth-mannered and amiable gentlemen. They would rather allow error to be preached , and souls to be deceived than hurt the preacher's feelings. Let Baal be worshipped rather than drought come! Let the cancer kill its victim rather than the cruel surgeon use the knife!...The best thing that could happen to some so-called Christian ministers of today is that they should be denounced in God's name by their hearers."

It is the treachery of silence when truth is on the scaffold and no one cries out against it.

Jesus Christ was not tolerant of evil. He denounced hypocrisy, "Then spake Jesus to the multitude, and to his disciples, Saying The scribes and the Pharisees sit in Moses' seat: All therefore whatsoever they bid you observe, that observe and do; but do not ye after their works: for they say, and do not. For they bind heavy burdens and grievous to be borne, and lay them on men's shoulders; but they themselves will not move them with one of their fingers. But all their works they do for to be seen of men: they make broad their phylacteries, and enlarge the borders of their garments, And love the uppermost rooms at feasts, and the chief seats in the synagogues, And greetings in the markets, and to be called of men, Rabbi, Rabbi. But be not ye called Rabbi: for one is your Master, even Christ; and all ye are brethren. And call no man your father upon the earth: for one is your Father, which is in heaven.(Matthew 23:1-9).).

Jesus denounced the church at Thyatira for allowing wicked woman named Jezebel to teach (Revelation 2:20).

Paul, too, was intolerant of evil, delivering Hymenaeus and Alexander to Satan, that they might learn not to blaspheme (1 Timothy 1:20)and labeling Hymenaeus and Philetus as false teachers (2 Timothy 2:17). Paul also And he reprimanded Alexander the coppersmith for his evil behavior (2 Timothy 4:14).

John also had the courage to name Diotrephes as one who loved to have the pre-eminence (3 John 9). It seems that the church today has lost its capacity for godly intolerance.

We hae been tolerant of anti-Biblical false teachings that have brought the church to the edge of destruction. If we play down harsh doctrines, we will gut our pleasant and comfortable beliefs.

The loss of the doctrine of hell and judgment and the holiness of God does irreparable damage to our churches.To preach the good news, we must preach the "whole counsel of God, including the bad news." But, in this age of tolerance, how?

Dr. Gagnon gives a very helpful diagram of these "exchanges" and "giving overs"

Stage 1: God's invisible transcendence and majesty are visibly manifested in creation (Romans 1:19-20).

Stage 2: Humans knowingly and thus foolishly "exchange" the true

Sinning Saints

God for idols (Romans 1:21-23, recapitulated in 1:25 and 1:28a).

Stage 3: God "gives over" humans to their desires/passions and to an "unfit mind" which aim at self-degrading and self-destructive forms of conduct (Romans 1:24, 26, 28).

Stage 4: Many humans then dishonored themselves by "exchanging" natural intercourse for manifestly self-degrading and unnatural intercourse (Romans 1:26-27); all engaged in some form of "improper" and evil conduct (Romans 1:28-31).

Stage 5: The self-degrading evil behavior to which God "gives-over" humans ends in the ultimate recompense of "death" (Romans 1:32).

Gary Ray Branscome declares, "One serious problem that we face in dealing with this error stems from the ambiguous nature of the word "tolerance." At one time that word meant essentially the same thing as hating the sin, but not the sinner. However, the anti-Christian element in our society now portrays all who condemn sin as intolerant, and that is where Christians must draw the line. Because people must see their sin before they will be able to see their need for a Savior, condemning sin goes hand in hand with bringing people to Christ. That being the case, love requires us to condemn every evil, including adultery and homosexuality, while those who tell the guilty that they have no need to repent are guilty of satanic hatred."

Will your life be governed by inner principle. . . or outer pressure? You will have what you tolerate. There are two voices calling out to us today. One is the voice of tolerance, and the other is the voice of truth. At a recent funeral I heard someone say, "All of us are going to the same place — some of us are simply taking different roads with

Sinning Saints

different styles and different ways." That is the voice of tolerance. The voice of truth reveals the words of Christ, "I am the way, the truth, and the life. No one comes to the Father except through Me." (John 14:6)

The 'total--tolerance crowd is intolerant of the subject of "hell."

At the recent annual Beeson Pastors School, Kurt Selles, director of the Global Center at Samford University's Beeson Divinity School, led two workshops to discuss "Whatever happened to hell?" He asked how many of the pastors had ever preached a sermon on hell. Nobody had, he said.

The Rev. Fred Johns, pastor of Brookview Wesleyan Church in Irondale, Ala., said after a workshop discussion of hell that pastors do shy away from the topic of everlasting damnation. "It's out of fear we'll not appear relevant," he said. "It's pressure from the culture to not speak anything negative. I think we've begun to deny hell. There's an assumption that everybody's going to make it to heaven somehow."

By O.S. Hawkins writes, "Tolerance seems to be the law of our land, and today it has a different meaning than it did a few years ago. Tolerance used to mean that in America we recognized and respected others' beliefs without sharing them. Today tolerance means that everyone's values, everyone's belief systems, everyone's lifestyles, are acceptable. Tolerance today says that all truth claims are equal."

According to Dr. Robert Gagnon, this text is "the most substantial and explicit treatment of the issue in the Bible Romans 1:24-27 is

Sinning Saints

also the most difficult text for proponents of homosexual behavior to overturn " The truth is that these powerful words should instill fear into anyone contemplating a homosexual experience or already tragically involved in the lifestyle. The Apostle Paul makes clear that homosexual perversion is evidence that one is already under the judgment of God. In fact, this judgment includes the removal of God-provided restraints to human sexual desires. To persist in sin is to run the risk of being given over to it by God. Dr. Gagnon points out that Paul reveals three "exchanges" and three corresponding "giving-overs" by God, beginning in verse 23. Deceived men and women have exchanged (1) the glory of the immortal God for idols (v. 23), (2) the truth of God for (lit. "the") a lie (v. 25), and (3) natural sexual relations with members of the opposite sex for sexual perversion with members of the same-sex (v. 26). Corresponding to these tragic decisions, God gives man over to (1) sinful desires for sexual impurity leading to the degrading of their bodies (v. 24), (2) shameful lusts leading to sex acts contrary to nature (v. 26), and (3) to depraved minds to do what ought not to be done (v. 28).

How can we claim Jesus as our Lord and Master and not hate the things He hated? How can we claim to be His follower without publicly denouncing the things He denounced? We must be intolerant of evil.

Sinning Saints

9

ON FRIENDSHIP WITH THE WORLD
by John Wesley

"Ye adulterers and adulteresses, know ye not that the friendship of this world is enmity with God? Whosoever therefore desireth to be a friend of the world is an enemy of God." Jam. 4:4.

1. The words of St. Paul contain an important direction to the children of God. As if he had said, "Be not conformed to either the wisdom, or the spirit, or the fashions of the age; of either the unconverted Jews, or the Heathens, among whom ye live. You are called to show, by the whole tenor of your life and conversation, that you are 'renewed in the spirit of your mind', after the image of him that created you;' and that your rule is not the example or will of man, but 'the good, and acceptable, and perfect will of God.'"

2. But it is not strange, that St. James's caution against friendship with the world should be so little understood, even among Christians. For I have not been able to learn that any author, ancient or modern, has wrote upon the subject: No, not (so far as I have ever observed) for sixteen or seventeen hundred years. Even that excellent writer, Mr. Law, who has treated so well many other subjects, has not, in all his practical treatises, wrote one chapter upon it; no, nor said one word, that I remember, or given one caution, against it. I never heard one sermon preached upon it either before the University or elsewhere. I never was in any

Sinning Saints

company where the conversation turned explicitly upon it even for one hour.

3. Yet are there very few subjects of so deep importance; few that so nearly concern the very essence of religion, the life of God in the soul; the continuance and increase, or the decay, yea, extinction of it. From the want of instruction in this respect the most melancholy consequences have followed. These indeed have not affected those who were still dead in trespasses and sins; but they have fallen heavy upon many of those who were truly alive to God. They have affected many of those called Methodists in particular; perhaps more than any other people. For want of understanding this advice of the Apostle, (I hope rather than from any contempt of it,) many among them are sick, spiritually sick, and many sleep, who were once thoroughly awakened. And it is well if they awake any more till their souls are required of them. It has appeared difficult to me to account for what I have frequently observed: many who were once greatly alive to God, whose conversation was in heaven, who had their affections on things above, not on things of the earth; though they walked in all the ordinances of God, though they still abounded in good works, and abstained from all known sin, yea, and from the appearance of evil; yet they gradually and insensibly decayed; (like Jonah's gourd, when the worm ate the root of it;) insomuch that they are less alive to God now, than they were ten, twenty, or thirty years ago. But it is easily accounted for, if we observe, that as they increased in goods, they increased in friendship with the world; Which, indeed, must always be the case, unless the mighty power of God interpose. But in the same proportion as they increased in this, the life of God in their soul decreased.

Sinning Saints

4. Is it strange that it should decrease, if those words are really found in the oracles of God: "Ye adulterers and adulteresses, know ye not that the friendship of the world is enmity with God?" What is the meaning of these words? Let us seriously consider. And may God open the eyes of our understanding; that, in spite of all the mist wherewith the wisdom of the world would cover us, we may discern what is the good and acceptable will of God!

5. Let us, First, consider, what it is which the Apostle here means by the world. He does not here refer to this outward frame of things, termed in Scripture, heaven and earth; but to the inhabitants of the earth, the children of men, or at least, the greater part of them. But what part? This is fully determined both by our Lord himself, and by his beloved disciple. First, by our Lord himself. His words are, "If the world hate you, ye know that it hated me before it hated you. If ye were of the world, the world would love its own: But because ye are not of the world, but I have chosen you out of the world, therefore the world hateth you. If they have persecuted me, they will also persecute you. And all these things will they do unto you, because they know not him that sent me." (John 15:18, &c.) You see here "the world" is placed on one side, and those who "are not of the world" on the other. They whom God has "chosen out of the world," namely, by "sanctification of the Spirit, and belief of the truth," are set in direct opposition to those whom he hath not so chosen. Yet again: Those "who know not him that sent me," saith our Lord, who know not God, they are "the world."

6. Equally express are the words of the beloved disciple: "Marvel not, my brethren, if the world hate you: We know that we

Sinning Saints

have passed from death unto life, because we love the brethren." (1 John 3:13, 14.) As if he had said, "You must not expect any should love you, but those that have 'passed from death unto life.'" It follows, those that are not passed from death unto life, that are not alive to God, are "the world." The same we may learn from those words in the fifth chapter, verse 19, "We know that we are of God, and the whole world lieth in the wicked one." [1 John 5:19] Here "the world" plainly means, those that are not of God, and who, consequently "Lie in the wicked one."

7. Those, on the contrary, are of God, who love God, or at least "fear him, and keep his commandments." This is the lowest character of those that "are of God;" who are not properly sons, but servants; who depart from evil, and study to do good, and walk in all his ordinances, because they have the fear of God in their heart, and a sincere desire to please him. Fix in your heart this plain meaning of the terms, "the world;" those who do not thus fear God. Let no man deceive you with vain words: It means neither more nor less than this.

8. But understanding the term in this sense, what kind of friendship may we have with the world? We may, we ought, to love them as ourselves; (for they also are included in the word neighbour;) to bear them real good-will; to desire their happiness, as sincerely as we desire the happiness of our own souls; yea, we are in a sense to honour them, (seeing we are directed by the Apostle to "honour all men,") as the creatures of God; nay, as immortal spirits, who are capable of knowing, of loving, and of enjoying him to all eternity. We are to honour them as redeemed by his blood who "tasted death for every man." We are to bear them tender compassion when we see them forsaking their own

mercies, wandering from the path of life, and hastening to
everlasting destruction. We are never willingly to grieve their spirits,
or give them any pain; but, on the contrary, to give them
all the pleasure we innocently can; seeing we are to "please all men
for their good." We are never to aggravate their faults; but
willingly to allow all the good that is in them.

9. We may, and ought, to speak to them on all occasions in the most
kind and obliging manner we can. We ought to speak no
evil of them when they are absent, unless it be absolutely necessary;
unless it be the only means we know of preventing their
doing hurt: Otherwise we are to speak of them with all the respect
we can, without transgressing the bounds of truth. We are to
behave to them, when present, with all courtesy, showing them all
the regard we can without countenancing them in sin. We
ought to do them all the good that is in our power, all they are willing
to us receive from us; following herein the example of the
universal Friend, our Father which is in heaven, who, till they will
condescend to receive greater blessings, gives them such as
they are willing to accept; "causing his sun to rise on the evil and the
good, and sending" his "rain on the just and on the unjust."

10. "But what kind of friendship is it which we may not have with the
world? May we not converse with ungodly men at all?
Ought we wholly to avoid their company?" By no means. The
contrary of this has been allowed already. If we were not to
converse with them at all, "we must needs go out of the world." Then
we could not show them those offices of kindness which
have been already mentioned. We may, doubtless, converse with
them, First, on business; in the various purposes of this life,
according to that station therein, wherein the providence of God has

Sinning Saints

placed us; Secondly, when courtesy requires it; only we must take great care not to carry it too far: Thirdly, when we have a reasonable hope of doing them good. But here too we have an especial need of caution, and of much prayer; otherwise, we may easily burn ourselves, in striving to pluck other brands out of the burning.

11. We may easily hurt our own souls, by sliding into a close attachment to any of them that know not God. This is the friendship which is "enmity with God:" We cannot be too jealous over ourselves, lest we fall into this deadly snare; lest we contract, or ever we are aware, a love of complacence or delight in them. Then only do we tread upon sure ground, when we can say with the Psalmist, "All my delight is in the saints that are upon earth, and in such as excel in virtue." We should have no needless conversations with them. It is our duty and our wisdom to be no oftener and no longer with them than is strictly necessary. And during the whole time we have need to remember and follow the example of him that said, "I kept my mouth as it were with a bridle while the ungodly was in my sight." We should enter into no sort of connexion with them, farther than is absolutely necessary. When Jehoshaphat forgot this, and formed a connexion with Ahab, what was the consequence? He first lost his substance: "The ships" they sent out "were broken at Ezion-geber." And when he was not content with this warning, as well as that of the prophet Micaiah, but would go up with him to Ramoth-Gilead, he was on the point of losing his life.

12. Above all, we should tremble at the very thought of entering into a marriage-covenant, the closest of all others, with any person who does not love, or at least, fear God. This is the most

Sinning Saints

horrid folly, the most deplorable madness, that a child of God can possibly plunge into; as it implies every sort of connexion with the ungodly which a Christian is bound in conscience to avoid. No wonder, then, it is so flatly forbidden of God; that the prohibition is so absolute and peremptory: "Be not unequally yoked with an unbeliever." Nothing can be more express. Especially, if we understand by the word unbeliever, one that is so far from being a believer in the gospel sense, -- from being able to say, "The life which I now live, I live by faith in the Son of God, who loved me, and gave himself for me" -- that he has not even the faith of a servant: He does not "fear God and work righteousness."

13. But for what reasons is the friendship of the world so absolutely prohibited? Why are we so strictly required to abstain from it? For two general reasons: First, because it is a sin in itself: Secondly, because it is attended with most dreadful consequences. First, it is a sin in itself; and indeed, a sin of no common dye. According to the oracles of God, friendship with the world is no less than spiritual adultery. All who are guilty of it are addressed by the Holy Ghost in those terms: "Ye adulterers and adulteresses." It is plainly violating of our marriage contract with God, by loving the creature more than the Creator; in flat contradiction to that kind command, "My son, give me thine heart."

14. It is a sin of the most heinous nature, as not only implying ignorance of God, and forgetfulness of him, or inattention to him, but positive "enmity against God." It is openly, palpably such. "Know ye not," says the Apostle, can ye possibly be ignorant of this, so plain, so undeniable a truth, "that the friendship of the world is enmity against God?" Nay, and how terrible is the

Sinning Saints

inference which he draws from hence! "Therefore, whosoever will be a friend of the world," -- (the words, properly rendered, are, Whosoever desireth to be a friend of the world,) of men who know not God, whether he attain it or not, -- is, ipso facto, constituted an enemy of God. This very desire, whether successful or not, gives him a right to that appellation.

15. And as it is a sin, a very heinous sin, in itself, so it is attended with the most dreadful consequences. It frequently entangles men again in the commission of those sins from which "they were clean escaped." It generally makes them "partakers of other men's sins," even those which they do not commit themselves. It gradually abates their abhorrence and dread of sin in general, and thereby prepares them for falling an easy prey to any strong temptation. It lays them open to all those sins of omission whereof their worldly acquaintance are guilty. It insensibly lessens their exactness in private prayer, in family duty, in fasting, in attending public service, and partaking of the Lord's Supper. The indifference of those that are near them, with respect to all these, will gradually influence them: Even if they say not one word (which is hardly to be supposed) to recommend their own practice, yet their example speaks, and is many times of more force than any other language. By this example, they are unavoidably betrayed, and almost continually, into unprofitable, yea, and uncharitable, conversation; till they no longer "set a watch before their mouth, and keep the door of their lips;" till they can join in backbiting, tale-bearing, and evil-speaking without any check of conscience; having so frequently grieved the Holy Spirit of God, that he no longer reproves them for it: Insomuch that their discourse is not now, as formerly, "seasoned with salt, and meet to minister grace to the hearers."

Sinning Saints

16. But these are not all the deadly consequences that result from familiar intercourse with unholy men. It not only hinders them from ordering their conversation aright, but directly tends to corrupt the heart. It tends to create or increase in us all that pride and self-sufficiency, all that fretfulness to resent, yea, every irregular passion and wrong disposition, which are indulged by their companions. It gently leads them into habitual self-indulgence, and unwillingness to deny themselves; into unreadiness to bear or take up any cross; into a softness and delicacy; into evil shame, and the fear of man, that brings numberless snares. It draws them back into the love of the world; into foolish and hurtful desires; into the desire of the flesh, the desire of the eyes, and the pride of life, till they are swallowed up in them. So that, in the end, the last state of these men is far worse than the first.

17. If the children of God will connect themselves with the men of the world, though the latter should not endeavour to make them like themselves, (which is a supposition by no means to be made,) yea, though they should neither design nor desire it; yet they will actually do it, whether they design it, and whether they endeavour it, or no. I know not how to account for it, but it is a real fact, that their very spirit is infectious. While you are near them, you are apt to catch their spirit, whether they will or no. Many physicians have observed, that not only the plague, and putrid or malignant fevers, but almost every disease men are liable to, are more or less infectious. And undoubtedly so are all spiritual diseases, only with great variety. The infection is not so swiftly communicated by some as it is by others. In either case, the person already diseased does not desire or design to infect another. The man who has the plague does not desire or intend to

Sinning Saints

communicate his distemper to you. But you are not therefore safe: So keep at a distance, or you will surely be infected. Does not experience show that the case is the same with the diseases of the mind? Suppose the proud, the vain, the passionate, the wanton, do not desire or design to infect you with their own distempers; yet it is best to keep at a distance from them. You are not safe if you come too near them. You will perceive (it is well if it be not too late) that their very breath is infectious. It has been lately discovered that there is an atmosphere surrounding every human body, which naturally affects everyone that comes within the limits of it. Is there not something analogous to this, with regard to a human spirit? If you continue long within their atmosphere, so to speak, you can hardly escape the being infected. The contagion spreads from soul to soul, as well as from body to body, even though the persons diseased do not intend or desire it. But can this reasonably be supposed? Is it not a notorious truth, that men of the world (exceeding few excepted) eagerly desire to make their companions like themselves? yea and use every means, with their utmost skill and industry, to accomplish their desire. Therefore, fly for your life! Do not play with the fire, but escape before the flames kindle upon you.

18. But how many are the pleas for friendship with the world! And how strong are the temptations to it! Such of these as are the most dangerous, and, at the same time, most common, we will consider.

To begin with one that is the most dangerous of all others, and, at the same time, by no means uncommon. "I grant," says one, "the person I am about to marry is not a religious person. She does not make any pretensions to it. She has little thought about it.

Sinning Saints

But she is a beautiful creature. She is extremely agreeable, and, I think, will make me a lovely companion."
This is a snare indeed! Perhaps one of the greatest that human nature is liable to. This is such a temptation as no power of man is able to overcome. Nothing less than the mighty power of God can make a way for you to escape from it. And this can work a complete deliverance: His grace is sufficient for you. But not unless you are a worker together with him: Not unless you deny yourself, and take up your cross. And what you do, you must do at once! Nothing can be done by degrees. Whatever you do in this important case must be done at one stroke. If it is to be done at all, you must at once cut off the right hand, and cast it from you! Here is no time for conferring with flesh and blood! At once, conquer or perish!

19. Let us turn the tables. Suppose a woman that loves God is addressed by an agreeable man; genteel, lively, entertaining; suitable to her in all other respects, though not religious: What should she do in such a case? What she should do, if she believes the Bible, is sufficiently clear. But what can she do? Is not this
A test for human frailty too severe?

Who is able to stand in such a trial? Who can resist such a temptation? None but one that holds fast the shield of faith, and earnestly cries to the Strong for strength. None but one that gives herself to watching and prayer, and continues therein with all perseverance. If she does this, she will be a happy witness, in the midst of an unbelieving world, that as "all things are possible with God," so all "things are possible to her that believeth."
20. But either a man or woman may ask, "What, if the person who seeks my acquaintance be a person of a strong natural

Sinning Saints

understanding, cultivated by various learning? May not I gain much useful knowledge by a familiar intercourse with him? May not learn many things from him, and much improve my own understanding?" Undoubtedly you may improve your own understanding, and you may gain much knowledge. But still, if he has not at least the fear of God, your loss will be far greater than your gain. For you can hardly avoid decreasing in holiness as much as you increase in knowledge. And if you lose one degree of inward or outward holiness, all the knowledge you gain will be no equivalent.

21. "But his fine and strong understanding, improved by education, is not his chief recommendation. He has more valuable qualifications than these: He is remarkably good humoured: He is of a compassionate, humane spirit; and has much generosity in his temper." On these very accounts, if he does not fear God, he is infinitely more dangerous. If you converse intimately with a person of this character, you will surely drink into his spirit. It is hardly possible for you to avoid stopping just where he stops. I have found nothing so difficult in all my life as to converse with men of this kind (good sort of men, as they are commonly called) without being hurt by them. O beware of them! Converse with them just as much as business requires, and no more: Otherwise (though you do not feel any present harm, yet,) by slow and imperceptible degrees, they will attach you again to earthly things, and damp the life of God in your soul.

22. It may be, the persons who are desirous of your acquaintance, though they are not experienced in religion, yet understand it well, so that you frequently reap advantage from their conversation. If this be really the case, (as I have known a few instances of the kind,) it seems you may converse with them; only very

Sinning Saints

sparingly and very cautiously; Otherwise you will lose more of your spiritual life than all the knowledge you gain is worth.

23. "But the persons in question are useful to me, in carrying on my temporal business. Nay, on many occasions, they are necessary to me; so that I could not well carry it on without them." Instances of this kind frequently occur. And this is doubtless a sufficient reason for having some intercourse, perhaps frequently, with men that do not fear God. But even this is by no means a reason for your contracting an intimate acquaintance with them. And you here need to take the utmost care, "lest even by that converse with them which is necessary, while your fortune in the world increases, the grace of God should decrease in your soul."

24. There may be one more plausible reason given for some intimacy with an unholy man. You may say, "I have been helpful to him. I have assisted him when he was in trouble. And he remembers it with gratitude. He esteems and loves me, though he does not love God. Ought I not then to love him? Ought I not to return love for love? Do not even Heathens and publicans so?" I answer, You should certainly return love for love; but it does not follow that you should have any intimacy with him. That would be at the peril of your soul. Let your love give itself vent in constant and fervent prayer Wrestle with God for him. But let not your love for him carry you so far as to weaken, if not destroy, your own soul.
There may be one more plausible reason given for some intimacy with an unholy man. You may say, "I have been helpful to him. I have assisted him when he was in trouble. And he remembers it with gratitude. He esteems and loves me, though he does

Sinning Saints

not love God. Ought I not then to love him? Ought I not to return love for love? Do not even Heathens and publicans so?" I answer, You should certainly return love for love; but it does not follow that you should have any intimacy with him. That would be at the peril of your soul. Let your love give itself vent in constant and fervent prayer Wrestle with God for him. But let not your love for him carry you so far as to weaken, if not destroy, your own soul.

25. "But must I not be intimate with my relations; and that whether they fear God or not? Has not his providence recommended these to me?" Undoubtedly it has: But there are relations nearer or more distant. The nearest relations are husbands and wives. As these have taken each other for better for worse, they must make the best of each other; seeing, as God has joined the together, none can put them asunder; unless in case of adultery, or when the life of one or the other is in imminent danger. Parents are almost as nearly connected with their children. You cannot part with them while they are young; it being your duty to "train them up," with all care, "in the way wherein they should go." How frequently you should converse with them when they are grown up is to be determined by Christian prudence. This also will determine how long it is expedient for children, if it be at their own choice, to remain with their parents. In general, if they do not fear God, you should leave them as soon as is convenient. But wherever you are, take care (if it be in your power) that they do not want the necessaries or conveniences of life. As for all other relations, even brothers or sisters, if they are of the world you are under no obligation, to be intimate with them: You may be civil and friendly at a distance.

26. But allowing that "the friendship of the world is enmity against God," and consequently, that it is the most excellent way, indeed the

Sinning Saints

only way to heaven, to avoid all intimacy with worldly men; yet who has resolution to walk therein? who even of those that love or fear God? for these only are concerned in the present question. A few I have known who, even in this respect, were lights in a benighted land; who did not and would not either contract or continue any acquaintance with persons of the most refined and improved understanding, and the most engaging tempers, merely because they were of the world, because they were not alive to God: Yea, though they were capable of improving them in knowledge, or of assisting them in business: Nay, though they admired and esteemed them for that very religion which they did not themselves experience: A case one would hardly think possible. but of which there are many instances at this day. Familiar intercourse even with these they steadily and resolutely refrain from, for conscience sake.

27. Go thou and do likewise, whosoever thou art that art a child of God by faith! Whatever it cost, flee spiritual adultery. Have no friendship with the world. However tempted thereto by profit or pleasure, contract no intimacy with worldly-minded men. And if thou hast contracted any such already, break it off without delay. Yea, if thy ungodly friend be dear to thee as a right eye, or useful as a right hand, yet confer not with flesh and blood, but pluck out the right eye, cut off the right hand, and cast them from thee! It is not an indifferent thing. Thy life is at stake; eternal life or eternal death. And is it not better to go into life having
one eye or one hand, than having both to be cast into hell-fire? When thou knewest no better, the times of ignorance God
winked at. But now thine eyes are opened, now the light is come, walk in the light! Touch not pitch, lest thou be defiled. At all events, "keep thyself pure!"

Sinning Saints

28. But whatever others do, whether they will hear, or whether they will forbear, hear this, all ye that are called Methodists!
However importuned or tempted thereto, have no friendship with the world. Look round, and see the melancholy effects it has produced among your brethren! How many of the mighty are fallen! How many have fallen by this very thing! They would take no warning: They would converse, and that intimately, with earthly-minded men, till they "measured back their steps to earth again!" O "come out from among them!" from all unholy men, however harmless they may appear; "and be ye separate:" At least so far as to have no intimacy with them. As your "fellowship is with the Father, and with his Son Jesus Christ;" so let it be with those, and those only, who at least seek the Lord Jesus Christ in sincerity. So "shall ye be," in a peculiar sense, "my sons and my daughters, saith the Lord Almighty."

[text of the 1872 edition]
[Edited by Shawn Dae Riley and Amy J. Riley, students at Northwest Nazarene College (Nampa, ID), with corrections by
George Lyons for the Wesley Center for Applied Theology.]

CPSIA information can be obtained
at www.ICGtesting.com
Printed in the USA
FFOW01n2014110315
11696FF